Brough Superior
FROM 1923

Road Tests and Features from
The Motor Cycle, Motor Cycling
& Motor Cycle Sport

Compiled and introduced by C. E. Allen

BAY
VIEW
BOOKS

Published 1990 by
Bay View Books Ltd
13a Bridgeland Street
Bideford, Devon EX39 2QE

ISBN 1 870979 18 4

Printed in Hong Kong

Contents

Foreword

THE writings of two Brough Superior enthusiasts, friends and admirers of George Brough, predominate in this book. Dennis May was the wittiest motorcycle writer of his day. Probably of any day. The extravagance of George Brough's motorcycles, the big twins especially, found an echo in May's style. His graceful word play, with its unexpected and sometimes outrageous flights of fancy, was much relished by the manufacturer, who was himself no mean hand when it came to a spot of hyperbole, verbally or for the published page. Entertainingly, affectionately, Dennis May wrote about Broughs mainly in *Motor Cycling*, but also for *The Motor Cycle*, under his own name and the "Castor" byline from the late 20s to the years immediately after the second world war. It was much later, in the 1960s, when C.E. – Titch – Allen wrote a series of articles for the monthly *Motorcycle Sport* that endure as the definitive account of George Brough and all his works. Motorcycle works, that is, for G.B. was a versatile man. So informed and understanding of the great man's career as designer, rider, publicist, manufacturer is the Allen version that the writer might have been at G.B.'s side throughout the tumultuous years at Haydn Road, Nottingham. If George Brough emerges as something of a hero figure, then that is entirely appropriate for in their relationship Titch Allen retained much of a veneration for G.B. instilled by early study, from afar, of the man and his machines, which moved him to write, of a pre-war period: "I . . . would not have dared touch the hem of his Stormgard had I met him!" He would not, however, claim all the virtues for G.B. But the foibles which may be an inevitable part of a personality such as his – notably, perhaps, the fine tuning with humdrum fact in which he occasionally indulged while promoting the Rolls-Royce of Motor Cycles – dwindle into insignificance compared to his achievements. George Brough and his machines were, and remain, unique in the annals of motorcycling.

Cyril Ayton

Introduction

By any standards, George Brough was one of the most outstanding figures the motorcycle world has ever known. From many points of view he was the greatest. In a lifetime which spanned three important phases of motorcycle development, veteran up to 1914 and (as they were known) vintage to 1930, and then post-vintage, he became a legendary figure throughout the world as founder and leader of the exclusive cult of the Brough Superior . . . the Rolls-Royce of Motor Cycles.

The real measure of his achievement was that by life-long dedication to the cause of perfection he raised the status of the luxury motorcycle to the point of acceptance by nobility, aristocracy and even royalty, and the image of his own machine to equality with the Rolls-Royce car.

Brough Superiors were always exclusive because so few were made. By manufacturing standards a mere handful of perhaps 3,000. (The actual figure is not known because some records were lost during the war. Some estimates put the figure as high as 6,000 in the 20 years it was in production, still no more than a month's production for a large firm. I prefer the lower figure.)

The ultimate tribute to George Brough's genius is that so few machines achieved so much in the world of motorcycle sport and contributed so much to British prestige. Achievements out of all relation to their numbers.

In the formative years just after the first war George Brough was not by any means the only designer/manufacturer/rider, yet from the moment he announced his intention to market his own machine – the Brough Superior, so as not to be confused with the flat-twin Brough made by his father – he stood head and shoulders above the rest.

He planned and built his personal "ideal" machine while still on war work at Coventry at the end of the 1914-18 war after trying out over 30 different machines. It had a thumping great vertical-valve 1,000 cc JAP in a light frame. There was really nothing very original about it apart from the beautiful plated saddle tank.

His father, still living in the world of flat tanks though once a trend setter who had made a rotary-valve single and was then sold on the flat-twin theme, was not impressed.

George Brough takes his SS100 to the top of Stonedale in 1925. He claimed it was the last occasion on which he smoked a cigarette

G.B. on Old Bill at a 1923 sprint

Father and son were a generation apart in years and an age apart in motorcycling outlook. A gulf too big to bridge. Young George claimed his patrimony, his £1,000 share in the family business, and blued most of it on a plot of land in Haydn Road, Nottingham, and the erection of a single-storey building of prefab concrete. This humble building was to become a veritable shrine of an heroic cult. Before it was finished George built his first three or four machines in the garage of his father's house, assisted by another youngster, Ike Webb, fresh from military service.

Oddly enough George Brough did not think up the trade mark Brough Superior himself. It arose from a discussion over pints in a pub. A crony chipped in with the suggestion, "Why not call it a Brough Superior?" when George was stuck for a name. George's father was not best pleased. "I suppose that makes mine the Brough Inferior," he snorted.

The first Brough Superior advertisement appeared in November, 1920. It was written by George himself, as were all subsequent adverts, was right to the point and sprinkled with the motorcycle slang of the day, an idiom which was never updated and in consequence developed a Wodehouseian ring to it. A bike was a "bus", the throttle a "tap". The machine he referred to as an "atmosphere disturber". He did not deign to quote a price but within hours deposit cheques were pouring in.

In one bold leap George Brough sprang to the top of the motorcycle tree. By his personal prowess in races, trials and sprints he was to hoist his banner to the topmost branch. In this select field there was only room for one at the top and he was determined to stay there. Success attracts competition and soon others were copying his ideas and his methods. Always the opportunist, he made capital out of their attempts by quoting Kipling:

"They copied all they could follow
But they could't copy my mind
And I left 'em sweating and a'stealing
A year and a half behind."

He did so with innovations like the first prop stand, twin headlamps, crash bars, interconnected silencers and, of course, his exotic fours.

In all success stories there are points at which seemingly unimportant occurrences have profound effects. I do not think that when H. D. Teague, then Midland Editor of *The Motor Cycle*, summed up his road test of the first SS80 Brough Superior by suggesting that it was The Rolls-Royce of Motor Cycles, he thought more of it than a convenient and popular synonym for the superlative in the motoring field. Seized upon and manipulated skilfully by

George Brough, the arch opportunist and publicity man, it became an accolade beyond price. Every subsequent advertisement and catalogue bore it proudly, though he was always careful to attribute the quotation to *The Motor Cycle*.

Where George Brough differed from so many rider manufacturers was in the unswerving way he followed *his* idea of what a motorcycle should be. He did not allow his vision to be confused by the demands of experts, the trade, or the press. He built the machine *he* wanted to ride, tested it and developed it in competition until he had proved it and publicized it, and then made replicas for those who were of the same taste.

Through the models year by year, from the Mark 1, the replica of his own "special", to the Golden Dream which faded finally in the cold light of post-war conditions, you can in the evolution of the machine clearly follow the evolution of the man from the swashbuckling extrovert of the 1920s to the seasoned connoisseur of the 30s, and finally to the idealist dreaming of flat-four, shaft-drive super bikes.

The first Super Sports model was the SS80 which came out in 1923. It was a production replica of G.B.'s first personal racers. The Mark 1 type with its pre-war type engine had not been fast enough in sprints and hill-climbs, and was too gawky. So he built a lighter, lower model with a highly tuned side-valve JAP and set out to prove its capabilities at Brooklands in 1922, the only suitable racing circuit. His Brooklands career was short and sweet. He won a five-lap experts' scratch race and was reputed to have lapped at 100mph, but subsequently the beaded-edge front tyre left the rim at full chat and G.B. created something of a record for sliding on his backside. No matter, he had proved his point.

His second racer had a frame so light that it had to be strutted externally from ahead of the crankcase to the rear spindle to keep it from bending in the middle when the power was turned on. The engine, a side-valve 1000, was very special, the pet of no less than Bert le Vack, the JAP development engineer and record-breaker. It was the track-tested prototype of what was to be a production super sports engine. G.B. tuned it still futher. With the bottom-end guts of a side-valve and the top-end revs of an ohv, this was probably the most potent side-valve ever. It was nicknamed "Old Bill" after Bruce Bairnsfather's immortal first war Tommy. (Already G.B. had realized the publicity value of nicknames for everything.)

No grass grew under anyone's feet at Haydn Road. Before the copyists could produce a match for the SS80 G.B. had another trump card up his sleeve. Le Vack had finally developed the Val Page-designed 8/45 ohv to the tune of taking the world maximum record at 119.05 mph, a record which was to last for two years . . . and G.B. had seen to it that the tank was Brough Superior whatever the rest of the machine had been made up from (the forks were pure Harley Davidson). In this magnificent "world beater" engine G.B. saw the chance to realize his first great ambition in speed. A road-going motorcycle with BS refinement which would safely top 100 mph on the road. Sheer speed was not enough. It had to handle. By the time

G.B. had tried and tested it, it did handle.

This was the SS100 model which in 1925 was G.B.'s idea of the ultimate in motorcycling and a breakthrough to a new dimension in motorcycling. The SS100 had, for all its potential, lines of delicate grace . . . the lines of a greyhound. It was G.B.'s greatest triumph as a designer (to be fair, others helped in the design stage but his was the inspiration and the final word) and the line was perpetuated in every subsequent BS.

With the aid of Freddy Dixon he built himself a world-beater. It was an SS100 shortened a bit and fitted with the latest long-stroke JAP. Dixon developed it at Brooklands, doing 103 mph for five miles with a sidecar, and George then went to Arpajon in 1928 for a serious crack at the record then held by Baldwin on a Zenith JAP at 124 mph. His failure became another legend, a failure so magnificent as to achieve much of his object. He did 130 mph one way but a piston failed on the return run.

One-way runs didn't count officially but for all that he was for quite a while (until next year when le Vack took over the bike and the record at 129 mph) the fastest man on two wheels.

His fabulous fours, the one-off experimental jobs which stole the annual Show in 1927, 1928 and 1931, and again in 1938, were commercial failures which cost him a great deal of money but were such magnificent failures as to be publicity scoops. These fours, first an in-line vee, then a

A much-published photograph of BS-mounted Lawrence of Arabia talking to George Brough at the Haydn Road works in 1933. G.B.'s sticks follow a spill in the ISDT

straight four, next the twin-rear-wheel, shaft-driven Austin-engine machine (which did reach token production of 10), and finally the h.o. four, were symptomatic of a recurring dream which drove G.B. on and ever on in search of the ultimate motorcycle.

He believed, as long ago as the middle 20s, as did many of his contemporaries, that to reach finality in design and in acceptance by the greater public the motorcycle would have to have at least four cylinders, perhaps shaft drive, but certainly the silence and refinement of a car. Accordingly he felt, as leader of the exclusive class, that the BS should lead the way to that goal. I feel that he developed a split mind over his luxury fours. He felt he ought to make fours yet still hankered subconsciously for the rumbustious vee-twin with its rollicking good humour. He fell in love with a dream of four cylinders but his first love and true love was the big vee-twin. Never in any conversation did I detect a real affection for fours, only idealism. Get him talking about bikes and always be was away over the hills on a great big bounding vee-twin.

Of all the dreams the Golden Dream was the most enduring . . . and expensive. Conceived before the war with the expert help of H. J. Hatch, the former Blackburne designer, on the design side and Freddy Dixon on development, it had all the features of an ideal design, a real Rolls-Royce on two wheels. In essence a pair of flat twins mounted one atop the other with their cranks geared together, it should have been completely vibrationless, and with over-square dimensions it was very compact.

To put the Dream on the market would, it was estimated, cost £80,000-£100,000. The firm, expanded by war work, could now manufacture it completely, but that would have meant sacrificing a flourishing precision engineering business. The final snag was that materials could only be obtained on Government permit against the promise of export performance. G.B. could see, too, that the market for expensive luxury machines was dwindling. There was a new generation and a new scene which G.B. no longer understood and which no longer understood him.

It was the end of an era, the autumn of G.B.'s life, though he did not at this point give up altogether. Following still his four-cylinder dream, he negotiated for a time with Gilera for the manufacture of their four, with continental scooter manufacturers for the manufacture of a scooter . . . after riding many makes to assess them. The final decision to give up two-wheelers must have been a hard one.

I was a latter-day BS enthusiast who had never been able to contemplate a Brough before the war and, being brought up to be respectful to my elders and betters, would not have dared touch the hem of his Stormgard had I met him! But when "Old Bill" came my way and was duly restored after its lifetime of hard labour on the road, I had the temerity to suggest, through a mutual friend, that G.B. might like to see it again, might even like to have a ride.

After 36 years he jumped on "Old Bill" and blasted off in the manner born. No "What's this for?", no hesitant trial runs. "Wham" – just like that – leaving a cloud of dust and the reek of "R".

The letter I received afterwards was in priceless period slang.

"I thoroughly enjoyed my reunion with my dear old pal, 'Old Bill' . . . the 'kick in the pants' which you get when you 'turn up the wick' was there 'as of yore'."

There was an unforgettable outing with his one-off auto banking sidecar, he shouting rip roariously into the wind, me petrified as the sidecar aviated. It all began to happen, the Brough Superior Club was formed to carry on where the Vintage Club left off, he became the Patron, was in demand at rallies. The rumble thump of Broughs was heard again to the glee of the old-timers and the mystification of the new men. Flash bulbs popped again, articles began to appear in the papers. It was meat and drink to him and the gleam came back to his eye.

His last ride when, defying doctors, he rode Albert Wallis's Austin-engined outfit round Mallory on full chat at the Vintage Founders meeting created the final legend of his lifetime.

Intuitively he knew that was how his fans both young and old would wish to remember him. His memorial is the hundreds of very superior motorcycles cherished throughout the world and the fund of legends that endures with them.

A man well versed in Brough Superior lore once said that the Brough part stood for George and the Superior part stood for Ike Webb. An over simplification, of course, but a clue to the unique relationship of master and servant which produced the Rolls-Royce of Motor Cycles. George Brough provided the ideas, the inspiration and goal, but someone had to see those ideas carried out in the spirit and to the letter, and that someone was Ike Webb. George Brough was always in the limelight. Ike Webb,

A 1954 photograph of G.B. on BBBB, Barry's Big Blown Brough – more formally, the supercharged Brough Superior with which E.C.E. Baragwanath set a Brooklands lap record of 103.97 mph in 1933. Engine changes occurred in the late 30s

indefatigable as machine-builder, tester, repairer and general factotum in the early days and later a tower of strength as works manager, shunned personal publicity and remained in the background, always approachable and a staunch friend of BS owners the world over . . . a particular friend of Lawrence of Arabia.

They say that service in the Guards leaves a mark on a man for life. Ike Webb served in both the Grenadier Guards and the Royal Marines in the first world war and the marks stayed with him for life in personal discipline . . . his early rising, 6.30 am was his life-long reveille . . . and his ability to work right through the night if need demanded. But more particularly it showed in his steadfast loyalty to his employer and his dedication to the Brough Superior marque.

It explains more than anything the relationship between himself and G.B. To Ike the soldier, G.B. represented the commanding officer, a rank which G.B. could assume as naturally as his jaunty cap. Ike was the company sergeant major of the tiny task force at Haydn Road which overcame all the obstacles of limited resources to build the world-beaters. When war came again it brought a bigger challenge, and this time Ike led his augmented forces so well in the battle of war production that he was awarded the BEM.

The last big outing for G.B., at Mallory Park in 1969. "It created the final legend of his lifetime." Titch Allen is standing

Only when the final decision was made that no more Brough Superior motorcycles would leave the factory did Ike leave his post.

There were other touches of the soldier about Ike. He would never indulge in the human frailties of tiredness or boredom, never allow himself much display of emotion and never admit discomfort or pain. In his last few years he must have suffered greatly, without betraying it to his closest friends. And he had the old soldier's love of "scrounging". He scrounged the very planks which made the first work bench the Brough Superior works had. He scrounged the parts, paying for them afterwards, for the only Brough Superior he ever owned. He took an inordinate delight in scrounging odds and ends from trade reps and manufacturers, most of whom I am sure enjoyed the chance to say "thank you" in a way which he appreciated.

A lifetime's experience of dealing with customers made him a master of the diplomatic reply and a great debunker of anyone trying it on. Beneath his rather bluff, soldier-like manner was a choice sense of humour. One of the last things he did in connection with Brough Superiors was to make a tape recording for a visiting American enthusiast. The American quizzed him about the coupling gears of the Brough Golden Dream. Were the gears noisy, as on the Ariel Four? "They were completely silent . . . you could not hear the engine running," said Ike, and I am sure he said it with a perfectly straight face. *Titch Allen*

"S.S. 80"

What the Symbols on the Latest Brough Superior Mean. Results of an Arduous 800=Mile Test of a 60 m.p.h. Sporting Sidecar Outfit.

By "TANGENT."

TO own an "S.S. 80" is to occupy a very select niche in the world of wheels, for almost all motor cyclists admire the latest Brough Superior. To consider but a minor point, they have a poor eye for beauty of line who do not.

Often, however, their attitude is that of the Ford owner regarding a Rolls-Royce (before he has driven one). It costs too much, they argue, and the extra cost is not balanced by the better performance. And even if it is, nobody really wants a machine capable of doing what the Brough Superior will do.

I have always felt that this reasoning was faulty somewhere; after a strenuous 800 miles trial of the machine under discussion (with a sidecar attached) I am sure that it is.

There are two ways of looking at the price of the "S.S. 80" model:—(1) Compared with small cars, and (2) compared with other sidecars. Generally (1) is favoured. £30 more would buy a 9.5 h.p. Kensitas occasional four or a 7-27 h.p. Kruschen sports model. It is easy to reply. There is not a standard light car on the market at less than £500 that has a road performance equal to this £180 sidecar machine.

Compared with a Smaller Outfit.

Or take (2). My own 500 c.c. sporting sidecar is capable of averaging 30 m.p.h., for instance, from London to Nottingham—a journey I made recently to bring back the Brough Superior. The bigger machine appeared to be, and probably was, nearly 20 m.p.h. faster in maximum speed, so what the average might have been had the return journey been hurried is a matter for amazing conjecture.

Sheer speed, however, is but one of the charms of this much-talked-of motor cycle. It has many more, so many that the temporary user, like our Ford owner *after* he has driven a Rolls, becomes thoroughly dissatisfied with his permanent vehicle.

Early Impressions.

These generalisations forced themselves to be written first. Perhaps it would be more interesting if I described my experience in detail rather than thrust any conclusions on the reader thus early and in such emphatic manner.

Two things impress one immediately on taking over the machine. The riding position and the lay-out of the controls are faultless; and the slow tick over of the engine in neutral is almost unbelievably restrained. Thereafter sensation follows sensation.

A fairly wide ratio gear box was fitted, for the outfit was a works and trials hack. Running through the gears from low to top was merely a matter of form. The even acceleration from 5 m.p.h. to more than 60 m.p.h. on top made a gear box seem superfluous. As the burble of the exhaust changed to a purr the outfit gained speed, it seemed, as quickly as the driver could move the throttle lever open. One can only compare it with a steam engine.

Incidentally, the exhaust note deserves a paragraph to itself. Normally, I do not become enthusiastic about such matters, but the battle-cry of the special edition of the super-sports J.A.P. engine fitted to the Brough Superior is real music to the ear of any keen motorist. Not loud but very reassuring is the best I can do without the aid of a broadcasting station.

"S.S. 80."—

From Nottingham to Town there was no passenger. Despite this, and despite the light weight of the striking streamlined Montgomery sidecar, the outfit felt safer on the left-hand corners than many a weighted sidecar leaning hardly in on its machine. The steering was finger-light, and I soon found I could approach corners in confidence at a high speed assured of rapid deceleration and as rapid acceleration at a moment's notice.

One morning later in the week I collected a heavy passenger and some quite considerable luggage, and set off for the hills of North Devon. We did not start very early, but we breakfasted at Reading and we lunched at Bridgwater—160 miles from our starting point. And we hurried only between many stops—for various reasons unconnected with the machine. The same journey might have been accomplished on the average reasonably fast touring sidecar outfit in the same overall time; but it would have to have been practically non-stop, and then it would have been a rush; whereas on the Brough Superior it needed no special effort, and implied taking no risks.

Up and Down Single Figure Gradients.

In the afternoon we toured on to inspect the chief test hills of the Land's End Trial. For the bends on Porlock low gear was engaged—incidentally, also, the first gear change on a hill since taking over the outfit, which will convey much to those who know the neighbourhood. If I were not happier on a solo machine than on a sidecar, I should have attempted a second gear climb, and would, I think, have been successful.

The descent of Countisbury (1 in 4 near the foot) was negotiated solely by aid of the brakes (back, dummy belt rim; front, internal expanding; both, excellent). It may have been a foolish experiment, but I dislike using an engine (on top or indirect gears) as an auxiliary brake.

On Lynmouth prudence again overcame bravado and we slipped round the lower hairpin on low gear. But

Not only is the riding position extremely comfortable, but all the controls—including the rear brake pedal, as the picture shows—are so located that the rider need not change this position at any time.

the Lynmouth that revealed itself as the front wheel was set ahead again was not the Lynmouth I had previously known. Inwardly sore at being so cautious, I decided that an immediate change up was the only satisfactory salve. It was a barbarous thing to do, but it was effected in great style.

That day's was my first attempt at Beggar's Roost on a sidecar, and I had seen too many better drivers than I fail to think of heroics on the third and worst hill. Nicking in "low" well below the famous hump of 1 in 2 point something, we burbled up on a mere whiff of gas, without Parsons chains, without bouncing, and with the passenger normally seated— or, rather, well wedged—in the sidecar. To enable a comparative novice to trials sidecar driving to shine on such a hill as Beggar's Roost is yet another charm of a smooth-running engine with an ample reserve of power in a sensibly designed and controllable machine.

Countisbury on Second Gear.

After a leisurely tea at ever-charming Lynmouth we started back for Bridgwater. Obviously we simply had to climb Countisbury on second. We did and I have since heard that some who watched us had never before seen anybody make so fast an ascent—probably an exaggeration, for I had quite a lot in hand.

On garaging for the night the speedometer showed our day's mileage as 250. It will be agreed that the machine was tested under the conditions which the type of motor cyclist who buys it will use it. To say it came through with flying colours is hardly strong enough praise.

Early next day we accompanied the Land's End competitors back to Porlock. There was much traffic on the hill, and we perforce had to crawl round the first bend, but I changed up before the second. We parked a little way further up, returning later to continue our journey. Here Nemesis overtook us.

On restarting, the clutch refused to grip and it was not long before we discovered that the cork inserts in the sprocket plate had burnt out. I was particularly annoyed, because the breakdown is unfair to

A roadside halt for petrol demonstrates that the tank filler caps are sensibly large. Incidentally, this view gives an excellent idea of the handsome lines of the outfit.

"S.S. 80."—
the machine. To be truthful I must record it, yet to be fair I should suppress it. The paradox is easily explained. It was my own fault. My present "weekday machine" has a metal-to-metal plate clutch running in oil. One can do anything with it; no amount of abuse affects it at all. Bad habits thus encouraged become a subconscious part of one's driving. I realise, in fact I realised as soon as I smelt burning cork, that I had been abusing a much more delicate clutch transmitting the drive of a much more powerful engine.

In a future issue will be described an ingenious temporary repair that took us to Exeter, where Pike's garage promptly fitted new inserts.

On the homeward journey the clutch was used more thoughtfully, but this did not affect our average speed. There is no need to divulge figures, although I will say that I was rather pleased with our time for the first forty miles—driving with due regard for other road users.

It was 2.40 p.m. when we left Exeter; we had tea at Wilton, near Salisbury, and we ran 200 miles before stopping for the night. Previously I had a theory that only on a liberally tyred and fast solo machine could one maintain high averages over long distances in perfect comfort. Now I include at least one make of sidecar outfit.

Factors Responsible for Comfort.

Several factors are responsible for this ease of body and of mind. A Brooks cantilever saddle, very flexible Brampton forks—so efficient, in fact, that, although a great believer in B. & D. Stabilisers, I admit that even they are almost unnecessary in this case—an excellent riding position and an accessible rear brake pedal are perhaps the most important.

The speedometer fitted was probably not reliable—the hand usually went mad at "62"—but it must not be thought that it under-estimated The outfit has been timed to 63 m.p.h., and probably does 65 m.p.h.

Petrol consumption was fairly heavy, not strange under the circumstances. Under more normal touring conditions it should be exceptionally good, for the power-weight ratio of the outfit is extremely favourable. Oil—Speedwell White Ideal—also disappeared with some rapidity. I over-oiled; I always do on machines not my own. The lubrication system, it may be recalled, employs two separate sight drip feeds—one to the front cylinder, automatically operated by suction under the piston, and the other to the timing case by a handle-bar controlled pump. The second is in the nature of an emergency oiler for prolonged high-speed work.

Carburation and Easy Starting.

A new pattern B. & B. carburetter appeared to suit the engine very well. It could be used as an automatic instrument, although the pick-up at low speeds was improved by shutting down the air. Starting from cold, a matter depending also on carburation and, to a less extent, on plugs—K.L.G.s—proved as easy after one had learnt the knack as it was difficult before. The gear-change, Sturmey gate, needs no comment beyond that it is accessible yet out of the way.

The brakes, it may be repeated, are excellent; the rear has one of the most secure and positive adjustments yet noted on its type, but one cannot help thinking that if the fibre pad were twice as large as it is, it would wear twice as long. If I owned the machine I have an idea that a new pad would be required every 3,000 miles or so! Furthermore, the average Brough Superior owner is probably just as rough on brakes as I.

Otherwise, after nearly 800 miles—750 of them as hard as I cared to make them—I cannot find a point to criticise. At the finish every part was functioning as well as at the start.

Road Tests of 1924 Models

No. 17.—The S.S.80 Brough Superior Combination.

THERE are presumably people to whom pride of possession is an unknown emotion, but among motorcyclists at any rate, they are few and far between. Thus is explained the undoubted fascination which the S.S.80 Brough Superior exercises over the minds of the sporting (and most discriminating) portion of the motorcycling community, a fascination to which we must confess we are ourselves sometimes subjected whenever we have one out on test.

This no doubt is because the Brough-Superior is admittedly built to a price in exactly the opposite sense to that in which the expression may be used on most machines; in other words, its maker glories in the fact that it is the most expensive machine on the English market, secure in the knowledge that it is nevertheless excellent value for money, since it is built as a real attempt to reach as close to perfection as is possible under present conditions without thought of cost.

When recently we had an opportunity of covering round about 100 miles on the latest S.S. 80, we were naturally keen to discover in what respect the 1924 model improved on the already remarkable 1923 type. In spite of the act that the machine we ran was fitted with a sporting sidecar, we were quick to realize that the new frame thoroughly justifies its existence by reason of the decidedly increased feeling of steadiness and rigidity which it gives to the outfit as a whole.

Unfortunately, winter was upon us as we left the Brough works at Nottingham, so both throttle and brakes were treated with considerable respect in the first few miles of snow-covered roads. Knowing the power latent in the 8-30 h.p. J.A.P.

engine, we realized that a flick of the twist grip from one-eighth to one quarter throttle might produce as disastrous a skid as a too sudden application of the brake to the back wheel, should this be at the moment on an ice-covered surface. Soon, however, familiarity with the machine removed these fears from our mind, and in spite of the treacherous conditions we were able to give the machine its head.

Here, perhaps, we should say a word regarding the new twist-grip control, which, quite honestly, seems to be the

An imposing front view. The width of the bulbous tank is notable.

ideal, for a fast machine at any rate. We have at times heard many criticisms of twist-grip controls in general, none of which apply so far as our experience goes to the type fitted on the latest Brough Superior, for the motion required is just sufficient to be within the capacity of the driver's wrist. All parts are accessible, and there is no fear of breakage, since the actual control is carried out by piano wire.

Yet another new feature must also receive commendation, and that is the steering head damper, for during the morning portion of our run we found the steering somewhat liable to dither when we were travelling fast over the potholey roads which are to be found in the neighbourhood of the Mansfield coal district. At lunch time we inspected the steering damper, and finding that it was instantly adjustable without the use of tools, we screwed it up a trifle, and thereafter the steering was as perfect as could be desired. We have mentioned these details of the machine at some length because adequately to criticise the performance of the outfit as a whole is somewhat difficult.

The sporting sidecar, well loaded with passenger and photographic kit, does not suffice in the slightest to slow the machine to such a pace that it would be possible on a winter's day to say definitely what was its maximum speed. We can, however, assert with every confidence that we were travelling at well over the mile a minute mark on at least a dozen occasions during our run, in spite of the fact that not once did we have the throttle fully open.

It is often said that it is difficult to find a road in England on which one can safely travel at three times the legal limit without "road hogging." These statements, however, must be made by people who have in mind the 60 m.p.h. performance of some hotted-up small engine of the old days, wearily

Road Tests of 1924 Models (contd.).

A happy combination of power, beauty of outline, and finish: the S.S.80 Brough Superior.

dragging its way up to its maximum speed on an excessively high gear. Such a machine could not be ridden at 60 m.p.h. without bad road manners, but on a machine like the S.S. 80, however, matters are very different. The acceleration is so tremendous that high speeds can be reached in a very few yards without the slightest difficulty, and since the brakes are sufficiently good to match the acceleration, speed can be held much closer to a corner or cross-roads than would have ever been possible in the old days.

We would merely suggest in this connection that the rear brake pedal is a little cramped in its position, for there is little space between footrests, brake pedal and gearbox, with the result that at the beginning of our run we once or twice fouled some portion of the gearbox with the heel of our Hutchinson wader when we attempted to apply the brake. To be fair, however, it must be admitted that had some of the slack in the brake

The acceleration, of course, is phenomenal, particularly so on the machine in question, which happens to be the one which George Brough piloted successfully through the Colmore Cup, for it was fitted with a Binks Sporting Mouse trap carburetter, which, once we had mastered the somewhat tricky handling of the air lever necessary, proved unexceptional in its action.

The timing gear is quiet, piston slap is noticeably absent in spite of the aluminium pistons, and the balance, of course, is as perfect as could be desired.

The gearbox, a specially built Sturmey-Archer, with nickel-chrome gears and stiffened shafts, calls for no comment except the remark that the gear change is easy and positive under all conditions, while the clutch is sufficiently sweet and yet light in operation to make starting on top gear perfectly practicable, as we proved for ourselves several times.

It is perhaps needless to say that comfort is a pronounced feature of the machine, for the riding position is ideal, and the 3-in. tyres ensure road comfort. We would, however, have preferred to see shock absorbers on the spring forks, for there was undoubtedly a little front wheel bounce on bad roads which would have been cut out by such a fitment, and thus, to a slight degree, the comfort would have been even further improved.

Apart from this, we have no criticism to offer, for the design as a whole is so thoroughly well thought out that the machine may honestly be said to be a joy to its owner. As for those people who cannot understand how it is possible to sell a motorcycle and sidecar combination the first cost of which is considerably more than that of many light cars, we can only suggest that they try one, for the feeling of effortless power, combined with smooth, speedy travel, which such a machine as the S.S.80 affords, cannot be matched by anything on four wheels costing less than a round thousand.

Our test of the Brough Superior was carried out under Arctic conditions.

gear been taken up this trouble would not have occurred, since less motion would have been required to apply the brake, and the pedal in the upper portion of its travel is quite free from all obstructions. It is, moreover, of commendable size, and the whole of the brake gear for both front and rear wheels feels perfectly rigid, with an entire absence of that objectionable spring which is only too apparent on some machines.

Both brakes are, of course, internally expanding, and of such diameter that they should be almost everlasting.

The engine needs little comment; we have said enough as to its power, but perhaps we may add that main road slopes of 1 in 15 or 1 in 20 seem to slow it not a whit, but with all its speed and power it possesses also the inestimable merit of docility, and will tick over as slowly as could possibly be desired, and pull at slow speeds on top gear in a manner which is usually supposed to be peculiar to the soft "woolly" type of engine.

Perhaps the most "sporty" of all combinations: the S.S.80 and s.c.

LAWRENCE—MOTORCYCLIST.

One of the Most Famous and Romantic Figures of the Great War, Col. Lawrence, "The Uncrowned King of Arabia," is an Enthusiast on Motorcycling.

LAWRENCE of Arabia, otherwise Col. T.E. Lawrence, is unquestionably one of the most discussed men of our day, and also one whose character is least assessable by discussion. A romantic, something of a mystic, and at the same time a man of action, he represents an enigma over which other people never cease to speculate, but he remains a mystery and one that is never likely to be completely solved. A soldier whose deeds have made history, he has also shown himself to be an artist with a command of words. Altogether, a fascinating figure.

His great achievement was, as many will remember, his work amongst the Arab tribes during the Great War, when he united a number of warlike chiefs on the side of the Allies, the effect of which was to hasten very considerably the success of our arms in the Middle East. The work that he did in those years has been immortalized by his own hand in those remarkable works, "The Seven Pillars of Wisdom" and "Revolt in the Desert."

Since the war, in order to escape from the limelight of publicity, Lawrence has served in the ranks of the Royal Air Force and is now an Aircraftman, in a squadron stationed in India, under an assumed name.

Neither of Lawrence's books is accessible to the general public. "The Seven Pillars of Wisdom" is an extremely costly work, intentionally designed for circulation amongst a select few, whilst the smaller book, "Revolt in the Desert," is now no longer obtainable and second-hand copies are difficult to secure. The Press has, however, whetted the public curiosity in the author, and the account of him given in a volume just published by Jonathan Cape, Ltd., under the title of "Lawrence and the Arabs," will be eagerly devoured.

High Adventure.

Motorcyclists are, probably, amongst the keenest readers of books of adventure, and they will study with relish the many exploits of Lawrence that Mr. Robert Graves, the author of the new volume, sets out in such an able fashion. But his hero has a particular interest for all readers of this journal in that he is himself an enthusiastic motorcyclist. He took to motorcycling shortly after the war and made it his pet hobby.

Read this extract from a letter written by Lawrence to one of his friends:—"It's usually my satisfaction to purr along gently about 60 m.p.h., drinking in the air and the general view. I lose detail even at such moderate speeds, but gain comprehension. When I

"THE UNCROWNED KING OF ARABIA."
Lawrence with his last mount, of which he speaks with such enthusiasm. He is a keen advocate of the biggest of big twins for solo riding.

open out a little more, as, for instance, across Salisbury Plain, at 80 or so, I feel the earth moulding herself under me. It is *me* toiling up this hill, hollowing this valley, stretching out this level place. Almost the earth comes alive, heaving and tossing on each side like a sea. That's a thing that the slowcoach will never feel. It is the reward of speed. I could write you pages on the lustfulness of moving swiftly."

"Good Enough."

That is indeed well put, and it affords striking evidence of the fact that motorcycling is a real "he-man's" pastime. Coming as it does from a man who is something of a national hero, it should provide much food for thought to those who have hitherto despised our pet hobby, and sons who find their parents "difficult" on the motorcycling question might well insinuate "Lawrence and the Arabs" into the household for propaganda purposes. It should convert many an objector, for a game that is good enough for the "Uncrowned King of Arabia" is surely worthy patronage of any healthy young man.

The First S.S.-80 Spring Frame Brough-Superior Put Through its Paces.

THE idea of springing the rear part of a motor-cycle is not new. Many years ago machines were built which achieved this object in one manner or another, but costly or faulty design and sometimes manufacturing difficulties have driven most of them off the market. Some failed through over-elaboration, a multitude of small bearings giving rise to undue wear, whilst others were fitted with light springs which, being undamped, failed to keep the rear wheel clinging to the ground.

Many of the earlier designs were made solely for comfort, as road speeds were not then high, but as engine design has developed designers have been forced to pay attention to rear-wheel grip on rough surfaces and so another spring frame era has begun.

It is very like Mr. George Brough to be in the forefront with any new idea and, in collaboration with Mr. A. D. Draper, the spring frame Brough-Superior was evolved.

An S.S.-100 model has been available for some time now and was described in *Motor Cycling* some months ago, but the type under review is the new "Spring frame S.S.-80," which will, of course, figure in the 1929 programme. As can be seen from the illustrations on the opposite page the very rigid rear frame pivots on a large bearing (10 ins. long) at a point behind the gearbox and the tops of the seat stays are connected to a pair of links, similar to those used in front forks. The movement of these links is controlled by two coil springs and damped by large frictional shock absorbers.

The spring frame S.S.-80 Brough-Superior.

The whole arrangement is extremely neat and thus falls into line with other Brough-Superior products, which have always been noteworthy in this respect. The spring-frame model, incidentally, is only about 4 lb. heavier than the rigid-frame model; the machine tested —the first of its type—weighed 441 lb. ready for the road. This may sound a big figure, but actually it is unimportant except, perhaps, when man-handling, and even this is reduced to a minimum by the prop-stand under the left footrest. There is in addition a spring-up rear-wheel stand.

Once the machine is under way nothing could possibly be more simple to ride. It literally will not wobble, and throughout the whole of the tests described here the steering damper was slackened right off and need of it was never felt. The machine careered along over any type of surface, hitting pot-holes, ruts and cross-gulleys without the slightest sign of instability. Once, descending a long main-road hill at an utterly illegal speed, both hands were removed from the bars, which were violently struck at one end. The machine gave a slight lurch and immediately pursued a dead-straight course again.

Marvellous as are the steering qualities of the new Brough-Superior, the way in which the spring frame allows one to take liberties over appalling surfaces is even more wonderful. In order to give the machine as thorough a test as possible it was taken to a district where many of the roads are unmade, full of deep pot-holes and here and there have drain gullies standing several inches above ground level. A section was chosen about 300 yards in length as being the worst, and here tests were carried out. Previously, one or two cars were watched doing their best at about 8 m.p.h. in second gear. The first run, just to get the feel of things, was taken at about 15 m.p.h. in second gear. Everything was so easy that, gaining confidence, a return was made at 33-35 m.p.h. in top. The forks were bottoming on the very worst pot-holes and the sprung rear portion was extending to its full range of travel above and below the normal, but the rider felt absolutely safe and was certain that if need be the speed could have been increased still further. Another rider took over the machine and repeated the performance.

A run was then made over the same stretch standing on the saddle and gripping the bars lightly, merely to be on the safe side if the model should want to take charge. The machine was purposely steered for large gullies and manhole covers but it took them in its stride and the rider's apparently precarious position was absolutely safe. The heading picture shows the machine riding over a drain cover alongside which a colleague lying on the road made careful observations of the behaviour of both wheels. He stated that each followed exactly the contour of the cover and was free from any form of bounce. The severest bump did not cause the frame to ground.

Feet very much up on a rough surface at speed.

Another stunt carried out was to ride the machine fast over the same stretch with the legs stretched out horizontally without support, as shown in one of the photographs. The fact that the rider could keep his feet from coming into violent contact with the handlebars testifies to the beneficial qualities of the spring frame. Such a feat would be almost impossible on an ordinary machine. On the B.-S. it was child's play. In fact, great difficulty was experienced in finding something that *would* upset the motor. In the end we gave it up.

On heathland abounding in small hillocks it was quite happy. On "three-ply" cart tracks high speeds could be maintained, and even in deep sand it handled every bit as well as the best lightweights.

On ordinary main roads at low speeds the effect of the spring frame was not so noticeable, but higher up in the speed range a gentle floating sensation was experienced over irregularities that would have brought a rigid rear wheel inches off the ground. It was possible to take rough corners at speed with both wheels clinging to the ground in a manner calculated to make a leech envious!

When traversing extremely rough ground the dampers can be tightened with advantage. A spanner is provided for this purpose, but it was felt that a hand adjuster, as on some forks, would be more convenient.

All bearing surfaces in the spring portion are provided with grease-gun lubrication and are of ample dimensions, so that the wearing qualities should be good. In fact, an S.S.-100 machine has done 30,000 miles without any trouble.

No excuse is needed for making little mention of the rest of the new S.S.-80, as the spring frame is of prime importance. The 8-30 two-cam J.A.P. engine, the Sturmey-Archer gearbox and the brakes all behaved in an exemplary fashion. The engine was very silent mechanically. Other B.-S. refinements included a primary chain-oiler, prop-stand, headlamp dipper and a Klaxet horn.

Starting was at all times easy and the slow running called for high praise in traffic work, as the big motor would "wuffle" along on top at almost any speed and get away smartly without having to change down. Braking was very effective and the advantage of the rear wheel following the road contour instead of hopping about was immediately noticeable in this connection. The movement of the rear wheel does not, of course, affect the brake-control action.

This is a machine capable of giving the joys of motorcycling at their very best and one which cannot but help to enhance the good name which this famous marque has justly earned for itself.

These pictures show clearly the range of rear-wheel movement afforded by the spring frame. On the left is the rebound position; whilst on the right the springs are fully compressed, as under the influence of a severe bump.

"Touring" at 106!

BACK in 1929 Mr. Charles Hobbs, of the Markenfield Garages, Ltd., Guildford, bought a standard S.S. 100 spring-frame Brough Superior. Just as you or I might—in our more fantastic dreams. He ran it for a spell, but, unlike you or I, he was not satisfied. It wasn't fast enough!

Here was a pretty problem, if ever there was one. Could *nothing* be done to relieve the boredom of sitting behind a speedometer needle which never passed the 100 mark; the deadly sameness of touring in the eighties? Supercharging, possibly. But that would mean a much-modified frame layout, as George Brough himself affirmed. A bigger motor, then? Much more probable. So the engine makers were approached and the brains of clever S. M. Greening brought to bear.

To possess the fastest motorcycle on the road. That was the ambition of Mr. Hobbs. And to this end special cylinder castings, each of 575 c.c., were made, having an oversize bore, and giving a total swept volume of 1,150 c.c.

Cylinder heads, ports, flywheels, connecting rods—all were polished to the utmost, and certain vital parts lightened within ample limits of safety. Pistons giving a compression ratio of 8 to 1 were fitted and a Bosch racing magneto replaced the standard ignition-cum-lighting unit. Then a large-bore, twin-float Amal carburetter, similar to the old 1925 "T.T. Amac" and using a 375 jet, ousted the regular article. As to timing, it was found that no improvement could be made upon the maker's valve setting, but the spark took 47° of advance—a 7° increase.

With these modifications the engine peaked at 5,000 r.p.m., giving 57½ b.h.p. at that rate of revolutions.

"There is something in this furious eating up of space that exhilarates . . ."

"Castor" Describes a
Speed Fiend's Made-to-
measure Ideal — and
Celebrates the Passing
of the Speed Limit

" . . . A glance at
the counter. It shows
. . . well over 100 m.p.h. !"

" . . . We're in
second. I pull
the throttle
through a third
of its range
and . . . "

But with the attainment of the necessary power
against the brake the work of producing the fastest
road-going motorcycle in the world was only half completed. It must be geared right, for instance.

The question of gearing could be settled more easily
by calculation than by experiment, and it was thus
that the top ratio of 3.25 to 1 was arrived at, the
second and bottom gears of 4.10 and 6.05 to 1 being
automatically determined by the relation of the ratios
in the ordinary racing box employed.

Then there is a right and a wrong riding position for
every kind of going, and 100-mile-an-hour road work is
no exception. Two-piece "Pendine" handlebars with
a pronounced drop gave the necessary inclination to the
rider's body, and an exceptionally cunning mounting
for the saddle brought the riding height down to the
remarkable one of 26¼ ins. Such a relation of saddle

to handlebar cried aloud for high-up footrests placed
well aft and the robust B.S. "scrapping" rests provided
the answer. They were, in fact, quite ideal. It then
only remained to pad the tank top with a Moseley
Float-on-Air rest and fit George Dance grips, wherein
the knees might nestle, to attain absolute feather-bed
comfort.

To complete the description of the Brough's non-
standard features, I must mention a rev. counter driven
from the crankshaft and mounted just behind the
handlebar windshield. Narrow D-section wings (the
rear one bearing a Lycett pad), a duplex Pilgrim oil
pump as now worn in B.S. circles, plated chain guards
and plain fishtails in place of the "expansion-chamber-
or - other - device - suitable - and - sufficient" so highly
esteemed in the police force.

* 　 * 　 *

I am waiting at the end of a slightly undulating
stretch of road some five or six miles in length, smooth
surfaced except for a certain waviness close in to the
grass fringe, and not a million miles from Guildford;
straight enough to be ridden its whole length "flat" on
a fast machine in the ordinary sense of the adjective.
It is a crisp, sunny afternoon with a snap in the air
and traffic is reduced almost to vanishing point.

From the direction of Surrey's capital comes a deep,
booming sound, reminiscent, rather, of distant thunder
at first, but sharper, more insistent, as it approaches.
The source of this disturbance comes into view round
a bend and resolves itself into the great Brough
Superior, its lavish plating flashing in the rays of the
sun. It comes to a standstill where I wait, its rider
gives the throttle a last loving blip and shuts off.
Strangely silent it seems now.

"TOURING" AT 106! (contd.)

For a few minutes I am instructed in the ways of this Big Gun of the world of "touring" motorcycles. "Bottom gear's pretty high," I am reminded, "so you should let the clutch in carefully till you get the feel of things. Oh, and its "back" for retard. Don't give her more'n half advance till the revs. get up to two-thousand-five or so in top."

Mr. Hobbs warns me: "I shouldn't turn it up too much for the first run if I were you. She sticks on the road like tar and it's hard to get a real idea of your speed. Keep an eye on the counter, anyway. Three thousand in top is about '75' and another 500 makes it 88 or so."

"Okay, chief!"

A man-size kick. Silence. Another. Still no reply. Third time lucky, perhaps. Woomp! There she blows! Thanks, Moby Dick.

I wriggle down into the saddle and tuck a wayward coat flap into an inviting "George Dance." Comfortable? Certainly. No empty-stomach feeling with this Moseley lunch-supporter. Click!—into bottom. Easy with that clutch now. That's in. Now we're covering ground. Up through the gears. The counter needle hovers round the two-thousand-five mark and I bring the spark back to full advance; keep her at that for a mile or two and ponder that our speed must be somewhere above that sixty; and yet it seems almost as though I could get off and walk alongside. I sha'n't try, anyway.

A few minutes pass and the line of red brick villas which marks the end of that scrumptuous stretch is coming up to meet us. Better turn back, I suppose. H'm—the brakes work, too. That may be worth remembering.

Child's Play.

Remarkable how handy it is for a big 'un; a feet-up turn in the none-too-great width of the road is child's play, as long as the child remembers what his clutch and spark levers are for.

Now for a fast run back. Might try to test the acceleration too. Up to three thousand in bottom gear, a jab and we're in second. Now for it. O-Oooh! I pull the throttle through a third of its range in one fell handful . . . and revise my ideas about the causes of spinal curvature. I recover from my new position on the mudguard pad and, fascinated, watch the needle jerk its way up through the thousands: two; two-five; three; three-five—another stab at the tank-side lever . . . and once again an involuntary change of attitude.

But this time I stay there and, head down, flatten out behind the tiny windshield.

Ahead the road stretches out like a dark-streaked, slightly twisting ribbon; the landscape hurls itself towards me till it seems some huge and unseen force projects it. But what is that my eye has fixed on? A white object, perhaps a half-mile up the road, is waving as if in warning. I half sit up, ease the throttle for a fraction, but only to settle back a second later reassured. It is the A.A. scout who stands to duty where the only side road intersects that gorgeous straight. And he (good fellow) has scented "something up" and is giving me the come-along. A moment later I am passing him. A glance at the counter. It shows four-thousand-four, *or well over a hundred miles an hour!* But there is something in this furious eating up of space that exhilarates, banishes unwelcome thoughts of bursting tyres, and the scout's salute is not unanswered.

92 m.p.h. Hands Off.

There is another curve ahead. Of infinitely great radius, but every curve is a corner at this hurtling gait. Once more I slacken back till the lever lies along the bar—heel over . . . over, and straighten up again. Into another straight we merge, taking a line of unpleasant-looking waves with the steadiness of an ocean-going liner. A sudden thought—and vague memories. A hundred-and-sixteen-hands-off. George Patchett or someone, wasn't it? Gingerly I release the grips . . . raise my hands six inches . . . now a foot. She steers herself and I reflect a little miserably that my role is that of passenger more than pilot. Another downward glance and drop my hands again as I watch the needle top three-thousand-eight. Ninety-two hands-off is fast enough for me, thank you!

I sight the waiting figure of Mr. Hobbs and reluctantly bring his soul's-joy back to rest. He is grinning. "Like her?" he asks. Do I like her—I ask you! He produces a neatly written table in which m.p.h. are sitting opposite r.p.m.; runs a finger across the page—and stops at 4,400. Follows a few careful calculations, in which the predetermined "complement" of the rev. counter, tyre wear and fractional wheel spin are allowed for. *The speed was 106 m.p.h.!*

I get back to my song of praise. It is the finest thing I have ever sat across, I affirm. He takes the hint: "Take another run, if you like." I do. Several, in fact; each with a thrill of its own. Once a coat flap works free at about the hundred mark—is sucked into the air intake, and I experience an extraordinary sensation of being about to shoot over the bars. I wrench it free—and there is business as usual in the breathing department.

Again, a seemingly unconscious Trojanist drifts out towards the near-side bank as I prepare to pass him at what seems little more than fast touring speed—but is actually eighty-and-some. Yes, we had our moments, this Brough and I.

The 1,150 c.c. spring-frame Brough-Superior tested by "Castor."

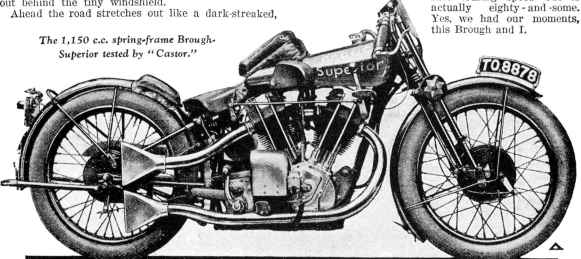

A STREAMLINED SUPERCHARGED BROUGH SUPERIOR
—Made Specially to Attack the World's Motorcycle Land Speed Record

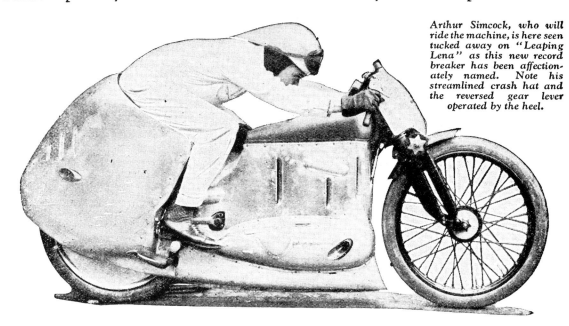

Arthur Simcock, who will ride the machine, is here seen tucked away on "Leaping Lena" as this new record breaker has been affectionately named. Note his streamlined crash hat and the reversed gear lever operated by the heel.

FOR five months past four Australians have been constructing a special Brough Superior machine to attack the World's Motorcycle Land Speed Record. These men are Arthur Simcock, who will ride it and is well known as a road race rider; Alan W. Bruce, who has made himself responsible for the mechanical side; P. E. Irving, to whom fell the task of designing the streamlined shell, and K. Horton, who has assisted in many ways.

Motor Cycling has known of the existence of the machine for some time past, but was asked to keep silent, and did so.

The nucleus of this latest speed monster is a "Pendine" model S.S.-100 Brough Superior. The wheelbase has been lengthened slightly to accommodate the Powerplus supercharger, which is held in a special cradle in front of the down tube. It has a pivotal mounting and the chain which drives it is adjusted by turning two long turnbuckles just below the steering head, which are connected to the blower casing by struts. The forks are of standard B.S. "Castle" type, but the blades have been faired off.

Constructional Details.

An o.h.v. J.A.P. engine, on which the quartette has spent much time, provides the power and has no fewer than four oil pumps. A fifth pump feeds the supercharger. A huge Amal carburetter supplies the mixture and K.L.G. plugs and a B.T.-H. magneto will be used. The drive is taken through Perrey chains, and there is a special Sturmey-Archer gearbox, giving three speeds but no neutral, and having a foot change operated by a reversed lever.

The specially made and balanced wheels take 28-in by 2.75-in. Dunlop tyres having ribbed treads. The Dunlop Co. have spent much time in evolving a cover which will stand the terrific speed which it is expected will be

A head-on view of the machine and rider showing the small area presented to the wind.

attained, and those fitted are estimated to have a life of 10 miles at 190 m.p.h. Each wheel has a short mudguard, and the rear is covered with an aluminium disc.

The tank is of standard Brough shape, finished in dull nickel, and has three separate compartments. The main one holds 1½ gallons of fuel (the consumption, incidentally, is 4 m.p.g.!), and the other two ½-pint sections carry oil for the chains and valve guides. All the filler caps are of the flush-fitting screw type. In the centre and slightly behind the small, dropped handlebars is a Jaeger rev. counter, which is so placed that it can be read when the rider is really down to it.

So much for the "innards." They are remarkable enough; but where this machine differs from others built for the same purpose is that a genuine attempt has been made at streamlining.

The Aluminium Shell.

Everything is enclosed by a sheet aluminium "shell" which has been specially beaten out by hand to Mr. Irving's design by Ewart's, of Euston Road. This body has been moulded around the rider, and the neat manner in which Arthur Simcock can tuck himself away can be seen from one of the photographs.

The covering is built up in sections around a steel framework, and each section is detachable, so that the engine and gearbox are not nearly so inaccessible as they may appear to be. The "tail" comes off as a whole and allows the rear wheel to drop out easily.

There are two bulbous portions low down on each side; they accommodate the blower drive and the cam box and oil pumps. Two small celluloid win-

In this view the bucket seat in which the rider sits can be seen, also the front fork fairing and the front cylinder exhaust outlet.

proved its worth. Its creators have been very reticent all along to make too much of a shout before the attempt; they prefer not to count their chickens before they are hatched.

It is hoped that this motorcycle, every part of which is British, will do somewhere in the neighbourhood of 165 m.p.h., but Simcock preferred not to talk of the matter in too much detail.

On Sunday morning last the Continental boat train steamed out of Victoria with Simcock, Bruce and the Brough all safely stowed away en

Keith Horton, Alan Bruce, P. E. Irving and Arthur Simcock standing behind the machine.

dows allow the rider to see that oil is circulating. Two short exhaust pipes come out flush with the sides of the body and along the sides also are vertical louvres to allow air to get to the engine and escape out of the tail again. There is a small opening in the very front to allow air to enter.

The workmanship put into the construction of this streamlined shell is really marvellous; there are hundreds of little copper rivets and any number of small screws, in spite of which the total weight is only 20 lb. At the top it screws into a flange around the bottom edge of the tank.

A terrific amount of thought and detail work has been put into this machine. As an example one may mention the little pump for replenishing the crankcase after draining; the handle of this protrudes through a hole in the casing just by the peak of the Dunlop saddle. There is also the name plate, a necessity when the machine is taken abroad, and that is made in one with the casing. There are numerous other examples to show the thoroughness with which these Australians have tackled their job.

Details of such things as gear ratios, blower speed and whatnot will not be disclosed until after the machine has

The rev. counter is mounted on a plate in the centre of the bars.

route for Tat, a stretch of road between Vienna and Budapest, 50 kiloms. from the later town. On Thursday (tomorrow) the Austrian Government will close 3½ miles of this perfect highway and every few yards along each side of the road will be placed a soldier. It is then proposed to attack the flying kilometre and flying mile records.

In order to get the machine ready in time there has been some really hard work put in, and many all-night sittings have taken place in the small room of a garage in North London, where the machine was built. If the attempt is unsuccessful it will probably be owing to lack of time to carry out detailed final tuning. On the bench the engine has shown enough power to attain the required speed easily, and it now remains only for luck to be kind to-morrow.

The "Overhead 500"

1931 MODELS ON THE ROAD

BROUGH SUPERIOR

The Brough Superior breasting a trials hill.

FOR more than ten years the big-twin Brough Superior has been the ultimate ideal of a very large number of really keen riders. Even those who have felt that its size has made it totally unsuitable for their use can hardly honestly say that they have never wished themselves able to afford something as imposing.

Then there is the other side: the desire of all real enthusiasts to own something uncommon, a machine of which they can be really proud. George Brough has catered for the select few by producing machines which, though "assembly" jobs, have personality, and in which each of the components has been specially made and tested.

Nevertheless, it is quite obvious that there are enormous numbers of riders who, for financial reasons, have never been able to attain their ideal. In answer to their cries, the less expensive "680" and "500" Broughs have been produced. These machines are still high enough in the scale for the owner to feel the same pride of ownership, though, naturally, they do not possess quite the charm of the "big stuff."

The interest of the 500 c.c. o.h.v. model, which formed the subject of this test, lies largely in the comparative rarity of the high-performance small vee-twin. The J.A.P. engine fitted is actually a somewhat de-tuned version of the twin which ran in last year's T.T.

SPECIFICATION.

ENGINE: 62.5 × 80 mm. (498 c.c.) J.A.P. vee-twin, with overhead valves.

IGNITION: Lucas Magdyno.

CARBURETTER: Amal, with twist-grip throttle control.

GEAR BOX: Sturmey-Archer four-speed. Ratios: 4.9, 5.9, 10.6, and 13.8 to 1.

LUBRICATION: Pilgrim pump, with auxiliary hand-pump (handlebar-operated). Tank capacity, ½ gallon.

TYRES: 26 × 3.5in. Dunlop.

FUEL CAPACITY: 3½ gallons.

WEIGHT (*in touring trim, with legshields, horn, prop-stand, electric lighting, and speedometer*), 418 lb.

PRICE: £105 *with standard full equipment; as equipped on test,* £106 10s.

MAKER: George Brough, Haydn Road, Nottingham.

---

races. Suitably geared, a machine with this engine should be capable of close on 90 m.p.h., though, for the sake of touring comfort, the standard ratio is 4.9 to 1; even so, the performance is greater than can possibly be used in the normal course of road work, and the machine can be cruised comfortably in the sixties. Using a speedometer as nearly accurate as is reasonable, the actual figures attained were 73-75 m.p.h. in third, and 80-84 m.p.h. in top gear. The steering was rock-steady at all such speeds, though some ripples on the road made it advisable to use the damper as a precautionary measure.

Seating himself in the saddle, the rider had the impression of being astride a big-twin rather than a five-hundred. The handling at all speeds was as delightful. A low riding position, a wide tank, and really comfortably placed bars all assisted in this important matter. No rain had fallen for one or two days before the test, and the various little hills picked out in Derbyshire were, consequently, comparatively easy. At the same time, the fact that they were climbed feet-up says much for the ease of handling of the Brough, when it is remembered that the machine was entirely strange to the rider.

The three hills were included in the Bemrose Trophy Trial, and provided widely differing types of going

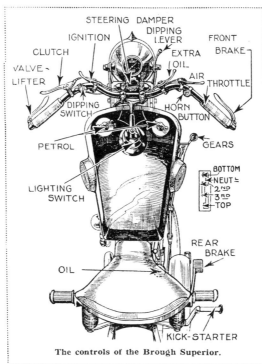

The controls of the Brough Superior.

Jackson's Lane, near Duffield, is a gullied, grass-grown climb, which can, as the Bemrose entry will remember, be very sticky indeed when wet. Lapidosa, and Gorsey Bank, near Wirksworth, are a mass of stones, the last-named being particularly rough. Jackson's Lane and Gorsey Bank were climbed in second gear (10.6 to 1.), but the extreme roughness of Lapidosa necessitated the use of the bottom ratio (13.8 to 1), though the grip had to be used with discretion when there was such a reserve of power.

On the road the machine cornered and handled really nicely, and only when negotiating sharp corners at the lowest speed was its size remembered. At first, there was a tendency for the rider to slip back, and this gave a feeling of personal insecurity, but it was soon cured by an alteration in the saddle angle. The small movement needed only goes to show the importance of slight adjustments in the riding position when complete comfort is desired.

Either brake would hold the machine, provided that the road surface gave sufficient grip, and both were perfectly smooth and immensely powerful in action. The long front brake lever, in particular, was a delight to use, and the pedal was conveniently placed, yet " out of the way."

Mechanical Silence.

Mechanically, the Brough was very silent. The gear box did not whine, slight valve rattle was barely noticeable at very low engine speeds or at the very highest, and the primary chain, enclosed as it is in an oil-bath case, might well have been absent.

To the rider the exhaust appeared to be rather more of a crackle than a burble at wider throttle openings, but it was an extremely pleasant sound. After standing by when another rider tried out the machine at speed, it was realised that no one could possibly call it noisy. Incidentally, after several runs had been made at full throttle, the exhaust pipes retained their pristine brilliance— perhaps the balanced silencer arrangement had a lot to do with that.

In spite of a compression ratio of

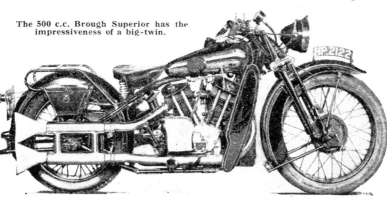

The 500 c.c. Brough Superior has the impressiveness of a big-twin.

7 to 1, it was possible to tick along in top gear at very low speeds when the ignition control was used with intelligence, the lowest smooth speed in this gear being in the neighbourhood of 12-13 m.p.h. with the ignition fully retarded. Starting was absolutely effortless, provided that the carburetter was not overflooded when the engine was hot.

Practically the only fault to be found in the machine was one which would largely disappear with use; the gear change in certain directions and between certain gears was stiff to work. This was particularly noticeable when dropping from top to third unless circumstances were just right, but with a sharp action it was always possible to move the lever, and the change was always silent.

The clutch was perfectly smooth, and very light for a machine of this size.

There was no opportunity of testing the weather protection, but the guards looked sturdy and efficient, and the legshields would certainly go a long way towards keeping the rider's legs dry, besides adding to, rather than detracting from, the appearance of the machine. No sporting rider could possibly take exception to these shields, either on the score of appearance or of reduced accessibility.

Running at a speed which was usually below 50 m.p.h., except for short bursts, the petrol consumption lay somewhere between 80 and 90 m.p.g.

Important Details.

Several small but important features, some peculiar to the Brough Superior, contribute to make the machine an exceptionally roadworthy one. First and foremost, there is the prop stand. Not once during the test was it found necessary to lift the machine on to its stand, a simple movement of the foot being all that was necessary.

For rear-wheel removal, part of the guard is detachable, being held in place by means of hand nuts. The positions of the lighting and charging switch, in the centre of the tank, and of the speedometer — well ahead of the bars—are both noteworthy. The whole machine gave that pleasant impression of being designed by an actual rider— which, in fact, it is.

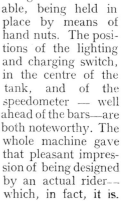

Solo Riding on
George Brough's Four

Hubert Chantrey on the London – Exeter Trial

BEFORE I had ever seen that marvellous new product, George Brough's latest masterpiece, the Straight Four, I had expressed my desire to enter the London-Exeter, if only for tradition's sake and the hope of a much-coveted Triple Award.

It came about like this. At the Show literally thousands were asking, "What is it like solo?" "Can it be ridden solo?" and one visitor, after asking to see Mr. Brough personally, explained that he would place an order at once if he could be allowed to ride the demonstration machine (which was outside Olympia with chair attached) solo.

The chair was accordingly detached and the machine taken down the Great West Road, where the visitor had only to ride the model for a few minutes before deciding to buy one.

So it was arranged that I should enter the Four solo in the Exeter, this having to be done at once since the entry list closed on the following Monday, December 7th.

George Brough promised to write me as soon as the machine was ready for collection; it was, in fact, the actual show model, no other being available as George Brough had entered the demonstration machine himself in the London-Exeter.

On the Tuesday before Christmas I called at the works to see about the model, and, to my delight, found it ready.

I may add here that I did not expect to be riding out on my Exeter mount when I arrived in Nottingham that morning, and, therefore, I had no motorcycling kit beyond a cap and a pair of warm gloves. However, it was all that was necessary for riding this well-protected machine. It was then getting dark, and I was a little nervous after having been called into the office and told that this particular motorcycle which was being entrusted to my care had cost its manufacturer well over £1,000 to produce as well as many weeks' hard labour, and,

therefore, I was not to have a head-on collision with the first trolley-bus I happened to meet (not that I am in the habit of having head-on collisions at all). Standing eyeing the model, I was almost frightened to touch it lest I should mark its beautiful finish.

However, my hesitation was overcome when the boss himself came along, bent over the model, pressed the button and the motor was started.

"Just try her up and down the road" calmly remarked the man whose mind had thought of nothing else for months, even years past. I did and . . . oh, boy, what motoring! I was on the new arterial type of road outside the works . . . dead level, few pot-holes, and practically no camber. In five glorious minutes I was convinced that twin rear wheels on a motorcycle were no different from one big one, at any rate for main-road riding. Up

and down the road I went, slow, fast, cornering, zig-zagging, hands off, first gear, second, and top. Then up a little cul-de-sac nearly opposite the works, all round the rough grass at the far end, but never having to take my feet off the boards. And so into the centre of Nottingham, where I stopped outside the G.P.O. to post a letter, and then back outside to the bike . . . but where was it? Gone? Yes. No. Crowds of people, twenty, thirty, if not a hundred, had gathered round. A touch of the starter button and I was off silently and with just a slight burrrr-burrrr from the fish-tailed exhaust.

Starting from Cold.

Birmingham was my resting place that night, and the next morning I was awake with the lark. How would she start from dead cold on a frosty morning? The usual car routine was followed—flood carburetter, hold strangler closed (this does not stay put), set ignition three-quarter advance, throttle slightly open, switch on, press button. Hurray! away she went, ticking over beautifully.

Soon I was at the Austin works at Longbridge, where I went to let Mr. Hancock have a look at the completed result of his part of the design. Great excitement was caused as I crawled round the various yards and roads inside the works demonstrating how nicely the machine handled.

There followed a general tour of Birmingham, taking the opportunity of calling upon other factories so that they might have an opportunity of seeing the latest in motorcycles actually functioning on the road—a thing Show models will not always do!

The ease with which one is able to place the model on its central stand surprised the technicians and designers everywhere.

Yes, one has only to press with either the left or right foot on the peg provided on the " roll-up " stand and steady the " barcycle " with one hand and she is up, no lifting whatsoever being required.

At the start of the London-Exeter Trial. H. B. Chantrey on the " Four " was the principal centre of interest.

Gently does it. H. B. Chantrey, the master of any big motor, showing the crowds on Harcombe Hill how delightfully his big machine handled.

On Christmas Day, after having ridden the machine about 100 miles, I left the Midland City at 2 p.m. for Torquay, a matter of over 200 miles. It was a lovely afternoon, and I can honestly say I have never enjoyed a run more than the beautiful trip to Bristol. The bike was behaving marvellously, and I certainly was able to forget the existence of twin rear wheels.

What the Doctor Ordered.

As I sped along, not exceeding 45-50 m.p.h. owing to a new motor, I thought how much less the present prejudice against motorcycles would be if they had always been as silent as this one. No valve clatter, no swish of chains, and scarcely an audible exhaust. Congratulations, my dear George. This is exactly what is wanted!

I found always that, on pulling up to inquire the route or for any other purpose, that I had *not* to stop the engine or bawl at the top of my voice to be heard or to hear what was being said. The tick-over is splendid, and I can only repeat the observations made by friends and acquaintances who are usually against motorcycles. " But it sounds and runs just like a car," they all said, and I can only qualify that by adding the word " good " before the word " car."

On arrival at Bristol we ran into a very thick mist, and, of course, had to stop frequently to gaze up at sign-posts. Under these circumstances, of course, the roll-up stand was an absolute boon. For several miles I was reduced to a crawl (15-20 m.p.h.), until I at last reached Bridgwater, where the air became crisp and clear once again.

After-dark Speed.

It was then that I was able to obtain the full advantage of a really efficient headlamp. The light given was certainly good enough for speeds of a mile a minute with perfect safety, and even more, although such speeds were not yet indulged in. And so to Torquay, where I arrived at 9 p.m.

After sorting out luggage, changing, and having supper, some dancing was a great success, and Boxing Day saw me off to some hills and rough stuff.

As before, the motor started on the first or second push of the button, and when filling up I noticed that 58 m.p.g. would certainly be a conservative estimate. The speedometer was not connected, the necessary drive from the gearbox not being available at the time of departure, and, therefore, an accurate figure was not available.

It was on the roads leading to

Higher Rill that I first felt the presence of twin wheels, as on the uneven roads, coupled with low speed, the machine wished to zig-zag according to whichever rear tyre happened to be the lower. This inclination to wander, however, was easily checked by a firmer grip of the wide handlebars and a determination to go straight.

After a while, and certainly during the Exeter trial itself, I had quite overcome this tendency. Higher Rill was climbed non-stop and feet up on the first attempt, despite the fact there were a quantity of pieces of rock secreted under the thick bed of leaves.

On Harcombe Hill.

Again on Harcombe I made a faultless climb, despite the mud and gradient, also on the first attempt. By then I was so satisfied with the machine's performance on rough stuff that I decided to ignore the other Exeter Hills and proceed back to London.

En route a lot of thick mist was encountered, which necessitated using the pilot light as an alternative to the brilliance of the headlamp. Presently, the small bulb "blew," and I duly dived down into the tool-bag thinking there might be a spare. What did I find? A very nice bag full of emptiness! I had come by then some four or five hundred miles without a single tool or spanner of any description.

I must explain here that I had unwittingly taken the machine from the works before the foreman knew I had gone for good, and, therefore, cannot attach the blame for this oversight to anyone but myself. And in any case the kit was not missed for the necessary spare bulb was soon found in the stop-light which is incorporated with the tail-light.

Preparing for the Trial.

Sunday morning came, and I decided my motor should be cleaned for the start of the trial. In under one minute I removed the two rear wheels, which were cleaned separately; this left the whole of the rear of the machine absolutely accessible, and, therefore, very easily washed down with a hose and brush.

The sump, the oil level in which had not changed since I left the works, was drained and fresh oil put in, about two quarts being necessary.

A grease-gun was applied to the various nipples on the Castle forks, and the water level was checked. The capacity is a little over a gallon, and the water never seemed to get really hot, although it was necessary to fill up with about a pint twice during the time I had ridden to date.

As for the trial itself, I need say very little, as this has been adequately described in a previous issue, but a word on the gear lever

and position of my hand on Harcombe would not be out of place in view of the various reports of an incident which occurred and was widely reported.

I arrived at the bottom of the hill in company with about No. 28 or 29. I was 44. I duly took my place in the queue of soloists awaiting the word "Go!" and when my turn arrived, as I thought, others (actually lower numbers than myself) were called up from behind by the marshal, despite the Club rule that "members shall proceed in order of arrival and not attempt to regain programme order"!

A few words with the marshal were of no avail so, seeing an opportunity, I attempted to proceed, unfortunately with first gear only semi-engaged. I had not proceeded far when the motor revved up and the model slowed down. Realizing at once what had happened, I snatched the lever and forced it back into bottom, having to drop my feet for an instant, and, so as to

leave nothing to chance, I proceeded for most of the way up the observed section holding the gear lever in and driving with one hand—all of which goes to prove how really tractable and easy to handle this remarkable machine is.

At the conclusion of the trial I handed the machine over to its maker, who was anxious to take it back to Nottingham to have its side-car replaced and delivered to its new owner.

I feel I must thank this lucky man for allowing me to ride the machine, and I am sure, when he reads this—my poor attempt to describe a wonderful motor-bicycle —that he will be proud to own a machine that has been so much in the public eye.

I can only add that I have since ordered one of these machines solo for my own use—both business and pleasure, and must thank George Brough for his pluck and endurance in giving us such an exquisite product.

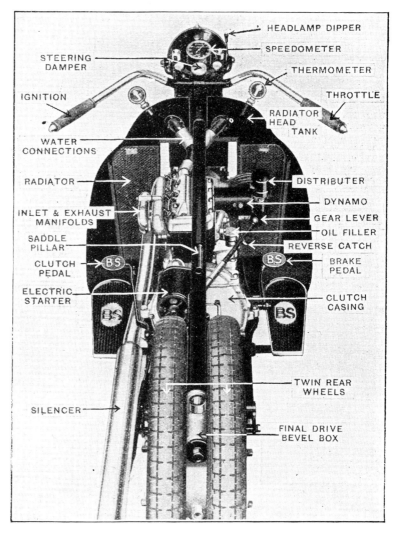

A close-up of the machine which H. B. Chantrey rode in the London-Exeter trial. The tank and saddle have been removed to show the details and the arrangement of the Austin-built engine.

*"*CASTOR," fastest-moving journalist on two (and three) wheels, serves it hot again! How the World's Fastest Sidecar Outfit was "road tested" by a member of "Motor Cycling's" Staff.

LENA TAKES ME for a RIDE

that *I* am counted in this rather untidy, quite unshaved and scarcely heavenly assembly.

No chant of praise is heard. Only a quick-fire rattle of conversation in the Australian tongue, with now and then a wisecrack and its laugh, while the stage is set for two minutes' pioneering in motorcycling journalism.

We are here that a World's Fastest may be "road tested." The machine is Leaping Lena, the Brough Superior combination which averaged 124 m.p.h. back and forth along the mile in Austria recently; I its rider-to-be.

Bustling hands remove an aluminium panel from Lena's covered-wagon sidecar; others cram gravel into the cavity of a sack which is destined, as passenger, to travel faster than most bags of gravel.

Bruce, in charge of the works, hurries to effect a change of plugs for warming up, and tells us simply, but with great force, how vexing it is getting at those works. "Wants a safe-breaker," he says to the little doors in the streamlining, reminiscent of speak-easy peep-holes, as they are set aside.

Two meadows distant a cowman, early bird of tradition, catches the worm with a monotonous "Coop, coop, coop!"; "and the same to you" seems the theme of the answering "Moo!" Meanwhile, idly, I drape my frame in the great adequacy of Alan's overalls (large men's, 35s.). The streamlined crash-hat, on the

YOU are familiar, I know, with that famous painting "Choir of Angels," which hung, faintly reproving, upon the bedroom wall of every child of pious parents. So that, had you chanced along a certain die-straight stretch of concrete by-pass, one recent Thursday's dawning, this symbol of a sound up-bringing might have been recalled by that which you had seen.

The same near-circle of earnest faces, corollaceous, hovering; the same roseate mistiness of the atmosphere, which comes only with a sun-shot daybreak. The same . . . but no, I think that there the similarity ends. For Cherub No. 1 is Alan Bruce, Australian motor-man of worldly fame alone. No. 2 is Phil. Irving, Australian, too, and motorcycle designer by profession. Next to him, Dave Brewster, six-foot gift of the Commonwealth to T.T. riding, with black eyes witness to his mortal birth. On the left Keith Horton, slide-car artist of the cinder circuits. "And friends"—as the fashion journals say—whereby you are to know

"... The grip is twisted on the most prodigious power producer ever the world of motorcycles knew—and things are happening ..." Lena, the Killer, at over 100 per.

"Leaping Lena," Alan Bruce's World's Speed Record Brough Superior, in an Ear-splitting Dash Across the Dawn

other hand, mocks my wide and noble brow by perching atop of it, ludicrously under-sized.

Right, then we shall have to do without it.

This is a "road test," so that you will want to know how easily Lena begins on chilly mornings. First, she breaks four tow-ropes, with a halt between each while the Choir of Angels condemns tow-ropes generally, and this one especially, to eternal and utter extinction. Then she is hauled a half-mile in silence, but for a whine from chains and "vacuum cleaner," to give the supercharger its technical name.

At length there is a spurt of flame and oil spray, accompanied by coughing reports from the foot-long double ports of the front cylinder. She is speaking! Another hundred yards and No. 2 cuts in, blending with the first in a roar more deafening than any two motors together that I ever heard. The very green-clad countryside, until now half-sleeping, seems to rouse itself into a questioning full-consciousness. What is this obscenity of sound, blasting so strangely into Hertfordshire's early morning somnolence?

Deftly Bruce unhooks the tow rope, locks her round in the road's width and drives back to where the gang stands waiting with a pair of *real* plugs, priceless things of cold blue and copper.

In the silence that follows on this warming-up you could hear a load of bricks drop. The grave, only graver. Alan's manly croak sounds like a whisper as he issues final orders:—

"The counter's not working, so don't bother watching it; anyway, I can tell what clip you're going, roughly. Hold on until you get Phil's 'All clear' from the other end, then let her have it." Adding, ironically, "Never mind about anything going your way; it shouldn't overtake you!"

A flutter of white, dimly visible through my goggles, perhaps a mile down the road. Let's go!

Tucked flat along that lean, live thing the sensation of the first hundred yards is one of being sucked forward by some force apart. It is that distance before the clutch is fully home, and twice as far before a pandemonium of shattering revs. sets me searching for the rear-placed gear-shift pedal. Got the brute! A stamp and we're in second, but only after a snatched glance down and back. (Disturbingly close together, those brake and gear pedals!)

Another lightning climb-up through the revolution range, until peak is not far off again . . . and Lena starts to Leap. And HOW she leaps! Sickeningly the sidehack wheel hits a lesser crater in the concrete, sending me six inches, a foot nearly, from the course I aim to navigate. Now the wind has got behind my goggles, bringing a blinding mist of tears. Nothing is quite distinct or distinguishable.

100 b.h.p.!

But this won't do. Shut one eye, you big goof, and keep the other screwed on that line of kerb! The noise is deafening, frightening, for, unlike anything else on wheels, the source of Lena's sound effects is out *in front* of her rider, where these evil-looking spouts jut shortly from her silver belly. Thus, the faster the more thundering comes that song of a hundred horse-power.

This, that's minutes in the setting down, is the deed of split seconds. The grip is twisted on the most prodigious power-producer ever the world of motorcycles knew—and things are happening.

Again my blurring vision must leave that narrowing grey-white line to look below and back, swifter than thought. Jab! That's top, thank goodness, and for the next few hundred yards it is just a matter of clinging on, as though to very life, and peering, searching through the mist of tears.

Always this has seemed a stretch that's made for boundless miles an hour. Lena, the Killer, knows differently, seeks out and revels in its vicious undulations, as she "takes me for a ride." She is master here, and knows it.

Ooch!—comes another lurch to starboard. Again that third wheel is inches off the ground, and the outfit turning everything but handsprings. Crack! goes the top connection against my port-side shin bone, numbing it momentarily.

Now, easy with the throttle, my gentle pansy. Here comes the curve at the end, negotiable at 80, perhaps 85, but not at this bat. The hazy panorama of the landscape resumes reality; there are trees and fields, and something which must be a human being. Probably an Australian; or would it be an angel, standing handkerchief in hand? Ah, yes—Phil Irving. Down into second at a steady 80 or so, for as Brucy cautioned me, you can't take liberties with these plugs; not the oily kind of liberty, at least.

A full-lock about turn, and back now towards the south. Blip! Blip! on the throttle, each twist to itself an inferno of crashing noise, each sending a fresh spurt of fire and reeking, half-burnt dope fumes from those gaping drains.

Yet, careful as I am, a tiny unconsidered blob of oil plants itself across the points of that back plug. Its work is done, and now as we return, a little ashamed,

LENA TAKES ME FOR A RIDE (Continued)

to the Choir of Angels down the straight, our coming is told by regular, single-syllabistic beats.

By contrast with the fury of power that was, this one-lung animal feels suddenly puny, as though scarcely it would pull a penguin off its nest.

"How's she gow'n?" chorus the unheavenly ones. "Gow'n good," my reply, "but short of sparks in No. 1." Unnecessary, this last, for before it is out of my mouth they are attacking the speak-easy doors with spoken word and screwdriver, a spare plug at the ready.

Two more tow-ropes twang taut and snap. The spoken word is heard some more. Even one that's new to me, a most expressive phrase. But insufficient, in all its glorious expressiveness, to will to the spot another tank of alky-fuel. Yes—it's empty! Five minutes before it was full to the filler caps—1½ gallons of Schneider plane stuff. About three miles that little lot took us!

"So that's that," from big Dave Brewster.

"And what was *that*—in miles per, I mean?" I query Alan W.

"About 105, I should figure by the way she sounded," I am told.

Slow, of course, measured by the record. But if anybody knows a good ploughed field, I'll see if we can better it.

Thanks, Alan. Thanks, Angels.

A BROUGH SUPERIOR WITH AN ELECTRIC STARTER.

FROM time to time in the past there have been various attempts to fit electric self starters to motorcycles, but the idea so far has met with little success. George Brough, however, has

cut-out are carried on a platform directly behind the gear-lever quadrant. A half-charge resistance is incorporated. This is fitted immediately below the main top tube of the frame, where it is

machine is in motion. It can, therefore be continuously coupled to the engine shaft; a chain running in an oil bath case is used for the purpose. The charging rate is 8 amps at 20 m.p.h.,

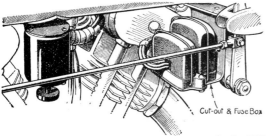

The neat arrangement of the B.S. self-starter can be seen on the right, whilst the left sketch shows the position of the cut-out, fuse box and switch.

Cut-out & Fuse Box

now got down to the job of fitting an S.S.-100 Brough Superior sidecar outfit with this equipment and has carried out a difficult and complicated piece of work with commendable neatness.

The idea originated with Mr. G. C. Howarth, of Sale, Cheshire, who, by reason of a "game" leg, was unable to start the machine.

A Lucas-type A1,000 dynamotor, measuring 11 ins. by 5 ins., is slung ahead of the front down tube on special forgings, and extra support is given by a strut connecting the dynamotor with the steering head lug.

The sidecar body is fitted with strong springs and a shock absorber so that it can easily take the extra weight of the large 12-volt 120-amp.-hour battery, which is housed in the locker. Heavy ¼-in. diameter cable is used to convey the current from this outsize in batteries to the dynamotor.

The switch is fitted underneath the tank in the space between the cylinders, where it is out of sight and yet can be easily reached, whilst the fuse box and

completely hidden by the saddle tank.

The dynamotor is, of course, an instrument which acts as a starter when the engine is stationary, but automatically charges the battery when the

and with a 36-watt bulb in the headlamp, 6-watt in the sidecar and a 3-watt in the tail lamp, the battery can just hold its own with all lights on at 18 m.p.h. The starter spins the engine briskly even from cold.

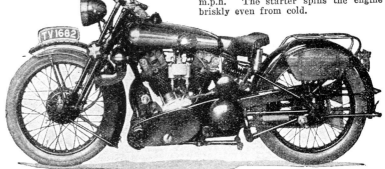

The S.S.-100 Brough Superior fitted with the Lucas dynamotor which acts in the dual capacity of starter and dynamo.

ALAN BRUCE TELLS HIS STORY

"Chair" Speed Record's New Holder On "Hanging On To The Works at 135 m.p.h."

IT'S a funny world.

And if you don't see anything to laugh at just think this over: in the last month my pal Arthur Simcock and I have made an aggregate of 130 hours railway travel, 200 kilometres by road and 12 hours on the water—just to set a record that was 58 seconds in the making all told!

But I am not complaining, having succeeded in something which has been on my mind since 1925, when I watched Paul Anderson take his Indian outfit down Sellicks Beach, South Australia, at 100 m.p.h. That gave me the germ of this big urge to go faster than the next best on three wheels. Then, four years later, the boat on which I and others of the Australian speedway bunch were making the trip to England put in at Port Said. Port Said only had one copy of *Motor Cycling*, so there was a fight—which I won. In that copy was the story and pictures of the big A.J.S. with which Baldwin was to attack the world's record. One look at those pictures and I was "rarin' to go." But, even so, it was another two years before Leaping Lena, our Brough Superior, had her being and made her first—and unsuccessful—series of record attempts in 1931.

Unaccustomed as I am . . .

If anyone has the idea that the life of a prospective sidecar record holder is spent in the saddle of an outfit, let them forget it. Up to the time that I took the world's figures away from Germany on April 30th I had not thrown a leg across an outfit since beating the track record at Wembley Speedway last autumn.

My job, here and now, is to describe to you what it feels like hanging on to the works at 135 m.p.h. or so. Therefore I need only be brief in telling how we fought tooth and nail against cruel circumstance during the days and weeks of our sojourn; how we went first to Neukirchner, near Vienna (where it was our original intention to make the drives), and suffered at the hands of some little ray of sunshine who had a steel bolt for disposal and dropped it into Lena's induction system! How Arthur, when within sight of the solo record, first had his goggles blown away and then lost the plot through the blower safety valve blowing off uninvited; and how we went from Neukirchner to Tat, many miles distant, having cajoled the Tat authorities into putting on a kind of private record meeting for our special benefit.

Then there was the furiously driven truck, Lena's (and our) means of transport, which blew up and arrived at Tat too late—and the further week's delay while "Simmy" rushed back to England for another blower and parts to replace those ruined by our Neukirchner well-wisher. Nor shall I ever forget the wonderful help and kindness given us by Eddy and Kent Meyer, the Vienna Brough agents, in our troubled days. If something wanted fixing, they fixed it.

1932 is Leap Year.

The record run itself was carried out under really terrible conditions, a strong side wind making it a matter of the utmost difficulty to keep the job along the dotted line (and that's about what that strip of concrete seemed like!). My worst moment came soon after the first kilometre tape, when the sidecar wheel struck a bump and the outfit came clear of the ground, being swept immediately to the off-side verge of the road. I had to shut off momentarily to fight it back, and the next instant, it seemed, came the second "big moment": unaware, in the big hustle, that I was well past the last timing strip I allowed the outfit to approach a level-crossing at speed. Bump! And what a bump! Again the whole thing shot in the air, and in landing split the lower streamlining and missed wiping off the carburetter by a fraction only.

Speed impressions are hard to put down on paper. But it certainly felt fast; which isn't surprising, since at 6,000 a minute, allowing a 7½ per cent. transmission loss, the speed must have been just about 135 m.p.h.

Yes, it *felt* fast all right!

Alan W Bruce

The author, Alan W. Bruce, flat down to it at over 130 m.p.h. An Australian achievement this, for not only is Bruce a "dinkum Aussie" but so is the sidecar, and the designer of the streamlining too.

"CASTOR" bids a sorrowful GOOD the

Letting loose something like sixty horse—and that means nearly 90-an-hour!

BELOW and without, dolls-housey from this seventh-storey window, stands a rank of many-specied vehicles. And at the end two cheap motorcycles.

One is a miniature-engined pop-gun of 148 c.c. The other is the Brough Sup. Howitzer which you see at the head of this column emerging from a bitter-sweet murk of Castrol gas at nearly ninety-an-hour. It would cost you, as it stands, perhaps £180. And it would be cheap, because there exists, I imagine, nothing else at the price upon which you and the passenger of your choice could capture the same thrill of rapturous gusty speed.

He says it's a Dying Species .... But Broughing—and Hughesing—at 87 m.p.h. fails to find the reason why.

These ultra-fast sidecar outfits are a dying race, it has seemed to me. The time was, seven, eight or more years ago, when they were a common sight along the roads: lean S.S. Hundreds of the late pre-chromium era, that sucked an exacting benzole blend through drain-pipe jets; now and then a bulbous, bold-fronted Flying Eight, clamped in rock-like unity to a T.T. Hughes—all strutted and stayed like a mobile Sydney Bridge. Or perhaps it was a Replica Norton, with padded rear and near-side wings and the single's tuny beat, that left you wondering . . . and wishing, perhaps.

Where are they now, these Big Guns of the sidecar world? The answer, in language of the telephone, is No Reply.

Perhaps, I thought, George Brough could tell me. Wrong again; he couldn't. But he would lend me what his letter called a " highly tuned S.S.100," which Ron Storey, the fastest man on sand, had cared for. Which left that friendly and resourceful sidecar trader, Maurice Wolston of Brixton Hill, to furnish a T.T. Hughes; and the human race at large to delegate a passenger.

This the human race accomplished easily, even if its representative was wont, as he said, to go to sleep in sidecars, and really I mustn't feel offended, etc., etc., etc.

Digressing, let me describe briefly the outfit as it stood at the setting out upon the most acutely wakeful ride in this passenger's career. One 8-55 long-stroke J.A.P. engine, with compression suited to 50/50 mixture of Ethyl Special. Four-speed box, with tank-side gear-shift, the three high ratios close and the fourth nowhere. Eight-inch brakes fore, aft and port. Three and a half gallon tank of Ethyl A, full measure, pressed down and almost running over.

Twin carbjectors, throaty, vacant-sounding chaps, pleasant to hear. Fixed at four firm points, one genuine Hughes basket, wherein basked one genuine human, two gallons spare Ethyl A, one quart spare Castrol " R," one gross British " Beech Nut " (permanent flavor—no, flavour).

Let's go!

Well, where? Fifty laps of Brooklands " road " course. Why not? For there, at least, there is nothing in the way.

Already I have tried to refute the theory that these big huskies are the playthings only of the Very Rich. Developing that theme, I will deny that they are for the Idle. There is no pastime less idle, and few, therefore, more absorbing, than lasting high speed on 700 lb. of sidecar outfit: this, verily, is work for the Worker, with a Chekha-Ogpu-Ogpu! Vive le Kamerad Marx!

*   *   *

At forty we are still in second gear—which please consider as bottom, and the box as a three-speed—merely warming up, hiccoughing asthmatically at every tenth beat or so. It is the noise of the twin calling for therms, which this afternoon, it happens, are scarce. Very well, then, little one, you shall have them in good time.

Presently, with two laps finished, the spitting becomes less frequent, until at length, with a last and petulant " choof " from the bell-mouth intake, like an obstinate child having the last word, she settles

BYE to ULTRA-FAST SIDECAR OUTFIT!

to it. Now the needle of the Jaeger meter is lying at a steady sixty; forward there by the tank nose the gear lever sits in the " third " position. Sixty in third —with basket and basker aboard!

But this is not the end. From the motor's feel, peak revs. are yet a long way off. More work for the throttle wrist . . . round, and farther round comes the grip to its full-stop. Simultaneously, the needle jerks on and up to sixty-five, sixty-eight, seventy. Still there are latent revs. in hand. Still there is power to spare. *And still we are merely in third gear.*

Seventy-two, three, three, three. Any advance on three? Going at three. . ... No, four. Seventy-four. Now five. Seventy-five—and peak. A flick of the wrist and the throttle goes backwards half a turn. A downward and forward jab at that gear knob . . . as quickly back to the bar again for that remaining half a turn. TOP!

This is good. Which reminds me, I wonder how the Human Being's nap is going. I steal a glance back and left quickly, fearful of disturbing him. What, awake? Yes, and clinging to the handrail like a fury. Raging insomnia, I wouldn't wonder.

Meanwhile, the meter shows a sure enough eighty-two, which, I reflect, is as fast as I have driven sidecars—unless you count Lena the Killer. So far, it is pleasant to ponder, the B.S. shows no signs of follow-

ing in Lena's finger-prints . . . none of the homicide stuff.

Eighty-three, eighty-four. Still that busy little hand moves round, a symbol, in its jerky animation, to the blast of power which propels it on its course. Eighty-five. Eighty-six. Eighty-seven. Seven . . . seven. No increase on eighty-seven. Here and there the surface is indented with long waves and ripples, nothing much at 50 per, but telling a different tale at nearly 90. Hop, skip, jump. The front wheel leaves the track and comes down not quite straight. Follows a dither, in which bars swing hard to right and left, trying hard to shake these wrists away. Half-lock to half-lock.

This *is* fun. But it's work, Karl Marx, it's work.

That fine right-hand sweep at the Members' Bridge. Not a thing in sight; just concrete, and a nice grass verge at the top of the bank, if it *should* be necessary. A snick into third, both hands on the off-side bar, a heave . . . and a long steady twist. For a hundred yards, perhaps more, we can hear above the rumble at the rear that squeal that tells of concrete *versus* tyres. Judged, if I may say so, to a nicety. May I say so? I glance down again to H. Being, Esq., telepathically inquiring. No! No! NO! seems to be the message of his answering glower. Now he is a martyr, I feel sure, not merely to wakefulness but to real alarm.

Next, a stop for plugs—pre-ignition, it seems.

" I say," he begins, " don't you think——" " Fish out those H.45s," I manage to get in edgeways. " Quick. Thanks. No, I don't think." Three minutes' feverish work and a burnt finger, over which we will draw a veil. (And a finger-stall.)

A rumble and she restarts, just in time to cut short another " I say . . ." Darn it, does the man want his motoring cellophane-wrapped, or what?

Right, right, right, go those never-ending corners. Always must there be a sufficient safety margin, yet

" It would cost you, perhaps, £180. And it would be cheap . . " You doubt it? Well, read what " Castor " says.

A17

GOOD-BYE TO THE ULTRA-FAST SIDECAR OUTFIT *(contd.)*

never a second lost. Truly it is hard work taking that right-hand "Villa" hairpin with this big handful. First a hefty prod at all three brakes as we approach the turn. Now harder on the rear wheel and simultaneously down a gear. The outfit answers our drag to port and reluctantly closes into the timing box, clear by the thickness of a shaving blade. Wallop!—on with the gas again just at the moment we're actually making the turn. *Drive* your corners —don't brake round them, which, I resolutely maintain, is the whole art of basketry. Sidecaring, I mean.

But it's Work, I repeat. (Apologies. I won't say it again.)

It is a broken primary chain that comes between us and the fifty laps. And having been chaperoned through life by a racing man this primary chain has no spring link, but only rivets, continuous performance. Nice and strong, of course; but when it breaks. . . .

* * *

Two hours passed before the welkin echoes to a gladsome "O.K., Chief." "Of course," says H.B., hopefully and (darn it!) with truth, "It's far too late now to finish schedule. Let's eat. And then let's just potter about the roads a bit."

We ate. And we rode many miles in the Surrey hills that day, ever regardful of safety, but setting some averages which made me glad that I was not alone, because two people's word are better than blank disbelief; and made H.B. profoundly sorry that I was *not* alone. How he hated me, the Brough and Life! And how I loved all three!

From experience gained that afternoon I would say that with an outfit such as this 55 m.p.h. could be safely averaged *ad nauseam* on a main road like "A.I." No, I didn't say that I had done so. Far from me be it, to use a difficult phrase. Certainly it could, though.

Yesterday, as ever was, we had a strange experience, the Brough and I. We, "and friend," were taking a long steady rise in Surrey and, being all clear, were travelling fairly quickly. *At the top those 700 pounds of iron and steel started to stand up on the back wheel.* The front wheel didn't hop off the ground. It just *climbed* into space. When it reached, I'd say, a two-foot elevation, I remarked the phenomenon, and thinking that something was due to be done, turned the momentum off in haste. Otherwise—well, I wonder. . . .

I still don't know why these big 'uns for two are a dying race. My ignorance is, indeed, aggravated. But that isn't George Brough's fault. Or that' of Maurice Woolston, of Elm Park Road, Brixton. Nor yet the Human Race's, bless it. To these, my salutations!

World's Record

Mr. George Brough on the record-breaking " Brough Superior."

Mr. H. Le Vack riding a

Brough Superior

with

STURMEY ARCHER SPEED 3 GEAR

put up a world's record at Arpajon of

130 m.p.h.

One more proof of Sturmey-Archer superiority. Specify it for your 1930 machine!

STURMEY-ARCHER GEARS LD., NOTTINGHAM.

DIARY of a THROTTLE TWISTER

JUST FANCY . . . . . . 106 *in*

MANY a witless whimscrack has started with the words Just Fancy, e.g.—Tramp No. 1: "Just fancy—a seven-course dinner, cigars and liqueurs, all for 6d.!" Tramp No. 2: "WHERE?" No. 1: "I've no idea, but just fancy."

*   *   *

THIS of mine is no mere variation of the theme. When I say to you: "Just fancy . . . 106 m.p.h. in second gear," I mean that in my capacity as Tall Stories Dept. I have just had the remarkable experience of riding a properly and legally equipped road-going motorcycle at 106 in second gear. Moreover, on a road (public not admitted, so there!).

The more elderly of my readers may remember

Alluring, sleek in its integument of chrome plate—the outsize B. ough-Superior tried by "Castor."

that early in 1931 one C. R. (and-what-a-man) Hobbs, of Guildford, lent me what was described as the world's fastest touring bike. I took it touring at around 106 m.p.h. No faster, because being at the time members of the public, Hobbs and I must needs use a public road, infested with Trojans, perambulators, waifs and strays, all eager to leave a wife and two children.

*   *   *

THIS time it was different. The road was different (closed). The bike was different (faster). Since last spring the compression of this 1,200 c.c. Brough-Sup. had sprung up to 8½ to 1. The cams had become more advantageously lumpy. Twin carburetters grew where once there was one. The valves were lighter.

The wizardry of Ted Baragwanath had been at work. . . .

Was there ever so Eureka-making a prospect? And yet my inward Eurekas were not unmixed with anxiety. I remembered this as the only thing on wheels which I had been scared to ride flat out. Now I dislike wearing my pride in a splint, and accordingly had made a silent vow to right the matter. And now here was Hobbs telling me that she should do her 120 on the just perceptible down grade of our stretch . . . which was neither

dead straight nor quite perfectly surfaced.

*   *   *

"I SHOULD go up the grade first if I were you. Just feel your way in second for the first run. Maximum revs. on that 4.42 second gear would work out at—er, let me see . . ." The speaker, C. R. (and what a man) Hobbs, broke off to consult a conversion table, raptly. "Yes, here we are, 6,000 r.p.m. equals 109.21 m.p.h. Try it, any-

way, and if you do get into top this run I shouldn't make the change above five-thousand-two. That's just 91." Nor should I. We have that much in common, have Hobbs and I.

So. . . . I was to "feel my way" at a paltry 106-per. Stap me! (and buy one).

*   *   *

WE haul her back against compression. Push a score of paces with the clutch up. Drop it—and she fires instantly with a tuny resonance through her Brooklands "official receivers." It is a moderate note, under this light warming-up load, yet having a quality suggestive of sublime immoderation, an insidious hint of boundless, prodigious power. Like a thunderstorm, distantly brewing.

I remember Moby Dick for the most caressingly comfortable of all fast motors. A Terry saddle nests low between the bolstered sponginess of pneumatic pads on tank top and rear wing. Scrapping footrests, high-placed and far back, throw the body

into a natural crouch, so that the postage-stamp absurdity which is the tiny windshield covers its subject handsomely. Always slight of build—like Gandhi, Charlie Dodson and other great men—my consciousness of puny stature is acute among these gleaming open spaces of chromium.

THE grip goes round a quarter turn. Click!—into second. Ahead there is the near-straight tarmac rise, beckoning its invitation to realms of speed beyond my ken. Below are nearly seventy brake horses. Right, let 'em come. . . .

Another sharp twist at the Binks quick-opener. With a bound—there is no other word—those five hundred-weights of iron and steel jut forward. Visibly she rises at the head, lifting the load from the forks until by its very feel I know the front wheel to be scarcely in touch with the tarmac.

Nestling behind the windshield is the white-faced rev. clock, translating into terms of tangible r.p.m. this

SECOND GEAR!

"Castor" Tells Another Tale of M.P.H. Sensations of Full-throttle Gear-changes at Over Ninety an Hour

phenomenon of mechanical science. Four thousand. In a breath to four thousand-five, five thousand, five thousand-five. Jerking, always jerking, that busy little hand works round. It fascinates strangely. I could watch it for hours. Yet I must tear my eyes off it and peer ahead at the smeary panorama of the road, and the banks that skirt that road. Yes, those banks . . . nasty things to hit.

Six thousand. Six thousand-one. The needle wavers, stops. The wind, seeming incredibly solid, strikes me like a rushing flood as I wriggle upward in my seat and ease back the throttle grip, gingerly, with reverent respect.

* * *

NOW down the grade, O Moby mine. Let us prepare to Go Places, as the Americans say.

The same lurching acceleration. The same large biff in the base of the spine, as reaction does its best to slide me off the back. Five thousand-two, saith the oracle, is gear-change time. And so it shall be. Watch it now. Four thousand-

eight. Five thousand. Five-one . . . now two. No declutching; this is a matter for the mag. cut-out, an ample black blob taped lovingly to the tank-side lever. I drop a paw from the off-side bar and fasten it on the lever and button. For a fraction, perhaps a fiftieth of a second, the power is cut off dead. There is a sharp, shell-like bang and twin

---

Next Week

Another "International" Machine to be Tested!

(Perrigo's B.S.A. is tested this week.)

---

tongues of flame show from the intake funnels. Simultaneously the gear slides in . . . and we unbutton the power.

If ever there was need to put hand to bar again it is now. A second ago seventy b.h.p., nearly, were screaming near to peak. Now, with not a whiff less gas, we are unbuttoning those gees on a gear a point higher.

THE SOURCE OF THE "SOUP." The rugged 1,150 c.c. J.A.P. engine of "the world's fastest road-going motorcycle," with its specially cast long-stroke cylinders, fed with Ethyl "A" through twin racing Amals.

YET apart from being all but left behind at the change-up, she steers and grips the road as surely as a freight truck. With this rear springing, pitching or wobble are non-existent, impossible. A feather bed could scarcely be safer.

The revs. climb up again, after dropping back with the extra top-gear load: four thousand-five. Now four thousand-eight . . . five thousand-two. Now I must screw an optic on the road again . . . and lay her over to make this scarcely perceptible left-hand curve. Hardly perceptible? Well, yes, when you're standing still. But this is different. Over she banks. A snatched glance back to that rev. clock. Five thousand-two.

Whoa there, Moby! She is straying out towards the off-side camber. Easy with the throttle, and over a bit more. Five thousand-two.

* * *

BACK to a standstill. Back to earth and the cold realities of a conversion table. "H'm—five thousand-two on a 3.5 top gear," says Hobbs, in a not over-enthusiastic tone, to thin air and his little book of figures. "That's 115.22 m.p.h. But you'll want to check the gear for yourself. The back wheel is 26 inch, of course."

Duly I check them. O.K.

Privately he thinks me something of a little pansy. He's probably right. But just to make quite sure, we have another crack at beating the figure. And another. And several more. But there's nothing doing. For, quite frankly, I don't like laying over too far on a doubtful camber at upwards of 115.

So Moby Dick is taken home, handcuffed and locked up again.

Just fancy. . . .

* * *

FREDDY DIXON sends everybody his love.

Too often when the great men of the riding game forsake our humble station for racing motorcars they develop a tendency towards an Oxford accent, *paté de foie gras* and roses round the door. Not so, Fred. Still he has a ready ear for the "short and simple annals of the poor," as I learned on Saturday night when he fell upon me with a Dixonian bellow in ye olde hostelrie a mile from Brooklands.

And just to show how interested he really was in all this cycling he adjured me please to remember when flying into print on the subject of Brooklands sidecar speeds that he, Fred Dixon, still holds the lap record. This is all very true, and very necessary, too, that you should know how true it is, since a theory seems to have sprung up in the latter part of the century that Ted Baragwanath's 103.11 is the record. "If you look it up," says Fred, you'll find my figure is as near to 104 as —— is to swearing." It is 105.9, which shows how close Fred came to using a wicked word.

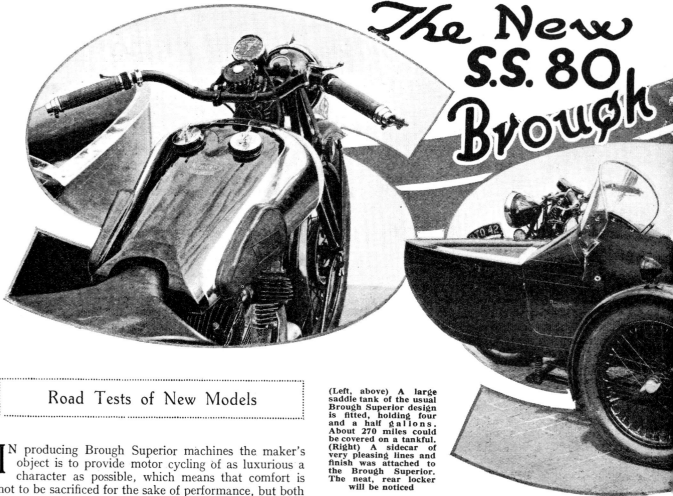

The New S.S.80 Brough

Road Tests of New Models

(Left, above) A large saddle tank of the usual Brough Superior design is fitted, holding four and a half gallons. About 270 miles could be covered on a tankful. (Right) A sidecar of very pleasing lines and finish was attached to the Brough Superior. The neat, rear locker will be noticed

IN producing Brough Superior machines the maker's object is to provide motor cycling of as luxurious a character as possible, which means that comfort is not to be sacrificed for the sake of performance, but both these qualities must be present to the highest possible degree. Behind the production of the new S.S.80 there is an additional object, and that is to provide a machine completely equipped and possessing all the Brough Superior characteristics but selling at a comparatively low price.

A big machine such as this has a peculiar fascination, and one cannot fail to be impressed by the performance. The sample tested was brand new and had been run-in only to the extent of one or two hundred miles. This being so, fairly gentle tactics were indicated, but, as it happened, there was the necessity of packing a lot of miles into a short period of time. The outfit was driven to its capacity on numerous occasions, but it did everything that was asked of it and, in many respects, exceeded expectations. The complete machine was by no means light; it scaled exactly 700lb. with petrol and oil.

When the performance figures are considered, in conjunction with the weight, it will be seen that they leave little room for criticism. Naturally, a high performance is expected from an engine of 990 c.c., but it should be borne in mind that the power unit is a side-valve with a compression ratio of only 5 to 1.

After a straightforward run from Nottingham to Birmingham the Brough Superior was taken out for a test of maximum speed. In top gear (4.97 to 1) a mean speedometer reading—on an instrument in which rather less than a 2 per cent. error could be detected—of 72 m.p.h was recorded with the sidecar empty. In third gear (5.97 to 1) the maximum was slightly over 60 m.p.h., while a speed of 51 m.p.h. was reached in second gear (8 to 1).

Under these conditions the steering was excellent; the steadiness of the outfit was truly remarkable, and control of the machine almost effortless.

The acceleration was also very good, the power of the engine and, incidentally, the faultless carburation, showing up well. In second gear the outfit took five seconds to accelerate from 20 m.p.h. to 45 m.p.h.; the time in third gear was approximately 6½ seconds; and in top gear, 8 seconds. These figures are surprisingly good, especially for a side-valve engine.

Fuel Consumption

The S.S.80 is a machine which invites one to drive fast all the time, and on roads reasonably free from traffic it was found that the normal touring speed was nearer 60 m.p.h. than 50 m.p.h. In spite of the comparatively high average speed which was maintained the outfit proved economical on petrol. An ethylised fuel was used, and an accurate measurement over 51 miles gave

Superior and Sidecar

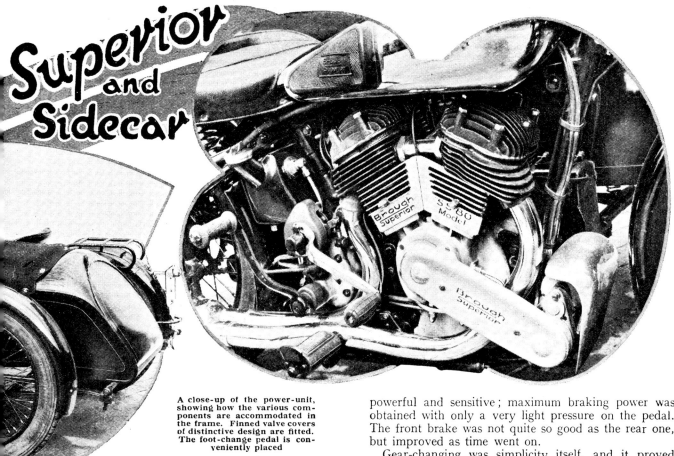

A close-up of the power-unit, showing how the various components are accommodated in the frame. Finned valve covers of distinctive design are fitted. The foot-change pedal is conveniently placed

a consumption figure of 60.4 m.p.g. at an average speed of 43 m.p.h. During the test the variation in the oil level was so small that it was impossible to measure the oil consumption with any accuracy, a fact that indicates that the machine was proving satisfactorily economical in this direction.

The engine was slightly on the rough side and its impulses could be felt at certain speeds. Low down in the throttle range no complaint was possible, but at about 45 m.p.h. in top gear a period crept in and could be detected up to about 52 m.p.h. Above the latter speed smoothness again reigned.

A Comfortable Mount

Road-holding was excellent—the fork action was good, very little steering damping was required and there was never any tendency for the outfit to proceed in any direction other than the one desired.

From the point of view of comfort the machine was well above the average, the saddle being an unusually large one of the pan-seat type, and the reach to the handlebars easy and comfortable. All the controls were handily situated, and the driver felt *in* rather than *on* the machine. On right-hand bends the steering was slightly on the heavy side, and tackling such bends fast involved a definite effort, though the steering was absolutely positive and free from waver.

The brakes were good, the rear brake especially being

powerful and sensitive; maximum braking power was obtained with only a very light pressure on the pedal. The front brake was not quite so good as the rear one, but improved as time went on.

Gear-changing was simplicity itself, and it proved impossible to miss a gear; the travel on the operating pedal was small, and the pedal itself was well located in relation to the footrest. The clutch, too, was good: it was very light in action and free from any trace of slip or drag.

Better lighting could hardly be desired, for the headlamp beam was long and wide, and permitted the full capabilities of the outfit to be exploited during night runs. The Altette horn had an excellent, low-pitched and audible note.

Altogether a machine of great charm, certain to please the big-twin enthusiast, and calculated to create enthusiasm in the rider who happens to be a stranger to the type.

SPECIFICATION

ENGINE: 85.5 × 85.5 (990 c.c.) side-valve vee-twin.

LUBRICATION : Dry sump, with oil tank on seat tube.

IGNITION : Lucas Magdyno.

CARBURETTER: Amal, with twist-grip throttle control.

TRANSMISSION : Chain. Primary chain in oil-tight case.

GEAR BOX : Four-speed, with foot-change. Ratios : 4.97, 5.97, 8 and 12.5 to 1 (sidecar).

TYRES : Dunlop, 26 × 3.5 in. front ; 27 × 4 in. rear.

PETROL CAPACITY : 4½ gallons.

OIL CAPACITY : 5 pints.

WEIGHT : 700lb. (with sidecar).

PRICE : (including electric lighting, horn and speedometer), £118 with sidecar.

MAKER: George Brough, Haydn Road, Nottingham.

THE 1,150 c.c., s.v.
BROUGH

A Luxury Spring Frame Outfit, Fast and Quiet

(Above and right) That the machine and sidecar are admirably suited to one another is shown in these two pictures of this very handsome combination, listed complete as depicted, at £162. The solo costs £130.

SYNONYMOUS with luxurious motorcycling is the name Brough Superior, and the latest "1150" with sidecar which we recently road tested is a worthy upholder of this fine reputation. It would be hard to visualize a more luxurious combination than the "1150" which took all ordinary roads in such an easy manner that both rider and passenger were able to arrive at the end of a long journey so fresh that they well might have been travelling in a luxury car. The sprung rear wheel levelled out the worst roads, and an effortless cruising speed of a mile a minute put the milestones behind one in a surprising manner. Anyone who was fortunate enough to occupy the passenger's seat had no hesitation in declaring the sidecar was the most comfortable they had ever been in. Good qualities which were still further enhanced by economical running—the all-in fuel consumption was 38-39 m.p.g.—and if 50 m.p.h. were not exceeded this figure improved to 46 m.p.g.

As comfort was one of the outstanding virtues attached to the "1150," we will state a few of the facts which were responsible for this state of affairs. To begin with, the sprung rear wheel and the bottom link front forks seemed to allow one to float over really bumpy roads at 60 m.p.h. when, on a normal rigid-frame machine it would have been prudent to slow down. No matter how severe the bumps, there was never any risk of the springs bottoming. Sometimes the rider would see an outsized pothole appearing and brace himself for the shock, only to find his forebodings were ill-founded.

Armchair Comfort

The riding position itself was rather like sitting in an armchair, the "pan" saddle being ideal for long-distance travel. One small criticism might be raised about the footrests, which were adjustable; in their highest position they were still a bit too low for our tester. Another ½ in. would have made all the difference. Plenty of variation could be made to the position

of the handlebars, which were clean, and long enough to make the steering light and easy to manage under all conditions. The clutch and air levers were the only ones of the "clip-on" variety, both front brake and valve lifter were of the inverted type, and the ignition timing was varied by a twist grip on the left.

Previous mention has been made of the comfort of the sidecar, but there were many other practical points which must appeal to the tourist. The locker, which opened front and rear, was big enough to house two small suitcases and a number of odds and ends. Provision was made for a really big suitcase by a grid mounted on the rear door of the locker. Easy access was another point; the squab was of the folding type and the door was wide and in the right place, so that the passenger, aided by the outside step, did not have to perform any acrobatic feats when entering or leaving the "chair."

An interesting and unique point about the sidecar is the chassis, the main member of which is a single large diameter (2-in.) tube running along each side of the body, round the tail, and over the nose. A filler cap is provided at the front and the aforementioned tube can be used as a spare fuel container with a capacity of just about 2 galls. To transfer the petrol from here to the tank, pressure is applied to a valve by the tyre pump, and a length of rubber pipe is connected to a tap at the rear of the chassis. The pressure forces the fuel up to the normal tank level. In addition, reserve taps are fitted to the normal tank which enable one to cover about 8-10 miles after the main supply runs out.

"Startability" was of a high order, one of the

TWIN CYLINDER
SUPERIOR
AND SIDECAR

(Above) Of original design, the chassis takes a roomy but sporting body. Our picture shows the transfer of the reserve petrol from the main tube to the tank. (Left) A head-on view of the outfit. Note the width of the handlebars. (Bottom, left) Seventy-two m.p.h. is a comfortable speed for this heavy combination, but the handling of the Brough Superior is well up to such performance.

snatch. During the course of ordinary touring it was quite common to find oneself burbling along in traffic at 10-12 m.p.h. without feeling any inclination to change down until acceleration was required.

Cruising at 60

It was a difficult matter to fix on any definite speeds for changing up or down, because the motor was so smooth and flexible that it was one's own mood which decided the method of driving. However, when travelling fast between one place and another the best results were obtained by changing from second to third at about **40** m.p.h. and from third to top at 45-50 m.p.h. A natural and comfortable cruising speed was just about 60 m.p.h. —a most creditable gait which made it *possible* to put nearly 50 miles into an hour, and *easy* to average 41-43 m.p.h. over a run from Kenilworth to the centre of Hull. For the potterer, or for ambling along narrow country lanes, the outfit was ideal, thanks to the light steering and delightful flexible engine which made life easy under these conditions.

When taken to the measured quarter-mile some good results were obtained, the best speed recorded was **72** m.p.h., and the mean timed speed was 68.18 m.p.h. In the low gears the best results obtained were 60 m.p.h. and 68 m.p.h. for second and third respectively. These figures rather indicate that for sheer maximum, top gear was a shade too high; however, it was about ideal on the road when full use was made of the close-ratio box. This latter remark is intended to apply to acceleration and hill climbing. About the only thing which was not in keeping with the general performance of the model was the front brake. Considerable pressure was required to bring about any result and at no time was it very

strongest points being the ease with which the big motor could be kicked over. Even when cold no particular effort was called for, and provided the carburetter was flooded and the air closed, first or second kick produced the desired result with the throttle opened just a shade. With the valve lifted, the ignition slightly retarded, the air open, and the throttle wound right back, one kick would start the big engine at a docile tick-over.

All-round performance was little short of astonishing considering the type of motor and the weight of the outfit, which was over 7 cwt. unladen. In top gear, with the ignition at about half retard, the "1150" would trickle along at a fast walking pace—too low a gait for the speedometer to record anything, so the speed must be estimated at 5 m.p.h. Further, by careful use of the controls, it was possible to accelerate away without any

Brief Specification of the 1,150 c.c. Brough Superior and s.c.

Engine.—60-degree V Twin, 85 mm. by 99 mm., 1,150 c.c. Side valves totally enclosed. Dry sump lubrication. Special pistons. Detachable cylinders and heads. Ports and combustion spaces polished. Forked connecting rods with roller big-end bearing. Lucas Magdyno. Twin float Amal carburetter.

Frame.—Loop frame. Rear wheel sprung on plunger principle. Bottom link front forks with four adjustable dampers. Rolling stand. Tubular

sidecar chassis with four-point attachment. 18-in. pan-type saddle.

Gearbox.—Four speed; positive stop; foot change. Extra long kick starter pedal. Pivot mounted for chain adjustment. Ratios (top three-close), 4.9, 6.0, 7.14 and 12.3-1. Primary chain in oil-bath.

Tanks.—Welded steel. Fuel tank chromium plated with black top panel lined in gold. Capacity 4 gallons. Two taps each with reserve. Oil tank capacity 6 pints.

Wheels and Brakes.—Wheels fitted with 7-gauge butted spokes. Journal ball bearings. 8-in. brakes front and rear. Dunlop "Speed" Universal tyres; 27 by 4.00 rear, 26 by 3.50 front.

Dimensions.—Saddle height 26 ins., ground clearance 5½ ins., wheelbase 57 ins., overall length 90 ins., overall width 62.

Tax.—£3 per annum.

Maker.—George Brough, Haydn Road, Nottingham.

Price.—Machine £130, sidecar with cruiser body £32. No extras.

---

much use as a stopper. The rear brake was excellent, being progressive, but capable of locking the wheel on any dry road.

The normal consumption tests were taken, 46 m.p.g. and 42 m.p.g. being the figures obtained in the country and town respectively. As previously stated, when high-speed work was indulged in, this figure dropped to 38 m.p.g. Oil consumption was most reasonable, only a pint was needed to "top up" the tank after a distance of 245 miles (1,960 m.p.g.). Whilst on the subject of oil, there were no external leaks either from the engine or gearbox and even at the end of 600 miles the mud could be hosed off the crankcase and cylinders.

Yet another feature which commended itself to our tester was the silence. Both mechanical and exhaust were exceptionally satisfactory, particularly the former, which was as good as that of any machine yet tested. The exhaust was subdued but when moving fast, with the throttle open, there was a healthy roar, not unpleasing to the ear, which gave an impression of sheer power.

Ease of maintenance was excellent, and all routine work could easily be carried out with the aid of the really comprehensive tool kit, which included a fine

selection of box and open-ended spanners, a point being that the job of adjusting the front and rear chains could be carried out in under a quarter of an hour. The tappets were easily accessible by removing the finned aluminium covers; whilst the machine was in our hands it was necessary to reset an exhaust valve clearance, an operation which took only 4½ mins. from start to finish.

Routine topping-up was no difficult matter with the fillers placed as they were. The best way of replenishing the oil-bath case was to tip the machine on to its offside footrest, afterwards restoring it to an even keel to determine the correct level.

A considerable amount of night riding was done which revealed the head light to be powerful and well focused. A detail which made particular appeal was the twist "dip switch" which was easy to operate, and which had the advantage of not relying on a spring to change from one filament to the other. The dynamo, horn and voltage control gave faultless service.

Taken all round, the "1150" and "B.S." Alpine sidecar made a delightful combination for all purposes. Priced at £162 complete it is an outfit which must be the ideal of many an enthusiast. The figure is high, but the value provided makes it well worth while—every penny!

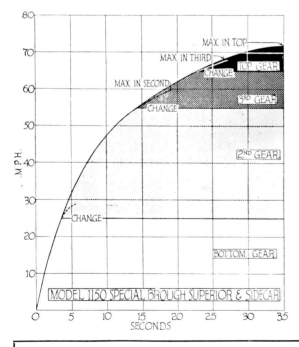

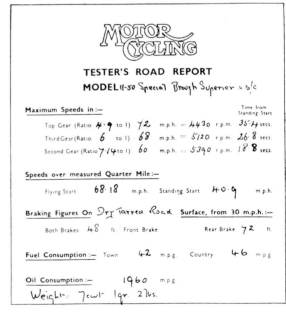

TESTER'S ROAD REPORT
MODEL 11-50 Special Brough Superior & s/c

Maximum Speeds in:—

				Time from Standing Start
Top Gear (Ratio 4.9 to 1)	72	m.p.h. = 4430 r.p.m.	35.4 secs.
Third Gear (Ratio 6 to 1)	68	m.p.h. = 5120 r.p.m.	26.8 secs.
Second Gear (Ratio 7.14 to 1)	60	m.p.h. = 5390 r.p.m.	18.8 secs.

Speeds over measured Quarter Mile:—

Flying Start 68.18 m.p.h.   Standing Start 40.9 m.p.h.

Braking Figures On Dry Tarred Road **Surface, from 30 m.p.h.:—**

Both Brakes 48 ft.   Front Brake   Rear Brake 72 ft.

Fuel Consumption:— Town 42 m.p.g.   Country 46 m.p.g.

Oil Consumption:— 1960 m.p.g.

Weight 7 cwt. 1 qr. 2 lbs.

THE EDINBURGH WITH GEORGE

By Henry Laird

The author astride the outfit which he tried out at the conclusion of the trial.

LAST year's London to Edinburgh found "yours truly" packed in a slim little banking sidecar outfit, with the inimitable George Brough astride the means of guiding and propelling said chair. A lusty side-valve engine made the trip a real pleasure, and afterwards left me wishing that the outfit was my own for "keeps."

This year George phoned me up some weeks ago, saying "What about our annual trip to Scotland?" "What about it?" I replied: "I have had the date booked for nearly 12 months." "Good enough," said he. "Have you any improvements to offer over last year's mach.ne?" To cut a long conversation short, it was agreed to take an S.S.100 with the latest Brough Superior chassis and sporting body.

Better Conditions

Last year, I don't think "the Master" had ridden in his own side-car, for he arrived at Stratford with nought but a well compressed and ancient hair cushion to insulate the passenger's lower dorsal curve from a somewhat hard metal floor. Good enough for a journey of 100 or even 200 miles, but not exactly the acme of luxury for nearly 800 miles in two days. The new body had all the latest conveniences included in the seating accommodation, to wit, a sprung back and a full-sized resilient seat. In addition, the floor was covered with a thick coconut mat, which, in conjunction with a toe rest, prevented the extremities of the feet making a noise like a Lewis gun on the metal body when traversing rough ground.

A Fine Model

Not being a lover of draughts down the back of my neck, I had the windscreen removed, wore goggles, a large coat and thoroughly enjoyed the fresh air rushing past my face. The machine itself was a typically George Brough looking piece of machinery with all the most up-to-date fitments. Bottom link front forks, a sprung rear wheel and a new front brake were salient points, whilst there is little need to enlarge upon the powerful 1,000 c.c. vee-twin engine, designed to provide the necessary urge of the right sort for the type of long journey before us. It certainly looked a lovely outfit and one of which the manufacturer-rider had every reason to be proud.

It was just beginning to get dark at 9.10 p.m. on May 26, when the M.C.C. official at Stratford told us, in schoolboy terms, "You may go now." And go we did! I was soon realizing what a grand sensation it is to travel in a good sidecar with a large 1,000 c.c. o.h.v. engine to propel one. The wind seemed to be rushing past and a glimpse at the speedometer dial showed we were cracking along at just over 60 m.p.h.

When we came to a hill, or needed to overtake anything, a flick of the wrist sent the needle round to 65 or 70 m.p.h. and the deep-throated burble from the exhaust changed to an unobtrusive but lusty roar. We trickled through Warwick, still in top gear, at 15-20 m.p.h.; even from this speed the acceleration was simply amazing, and there seemed little need to use the gearbox in ordinary circumstances.

First Stop

The dismal hour of 10 p.m. was almost upon us as we were drawing into Dunchurch, so, knowing that it would be the last for many hours, we halted and tried one! The crowd in the bar were in good song and full of the holiday spirit, so it seemed strange to leave this cheery company hoping to reach Edinburgh by 5.45 the next evening. However, George lived up to his reputation and was "off like a flash" through Rugby and Market Harborough. We stopped for fuel in Rugby and at one point George had an excellent chance to demonstrate the efficiency of his front brake, thanks to the road diving off to the right without the slightest warning. We took a wrong turn out of Market Harboro', but after a somewhat inebriated local "snent ush in the right direcshion" we arrived at Stamford, the first check, with time in hand.

After signing the sheet, we had sandwiches and tea before going up the Great North Road to Doncaster. George had been somewhat uncomplimentary about the sinuous road from Stratford and vowed that next year we would start from London; however, by the time we reached Doncaster my man had other ideas! The night traffic was terrible; lorries and numbers of private coaches were travelling in both directions, most of them with lamps like searchlights and an utter disregard for the dipping beam on the Brough. Nevertheless, we had time for forty winks outside the check and went on our way rejoicing in the thought of breakfast at the "Marquis of Granby," Harrogate, only 40 miles distant.

A really impressive-looking outfit with a performance in keeping with its appearance.

After being seated in the dining room for a minute or so, a waiter arrived inquiring, "What would you like to eat?" "Everything you have," was the answer, to which the waiter politely replied, "We normally only serve five courses for 3s. 6d., but if you care to pay extra you can have as much as you like." Believe me, 3s. 6d. purchased all we needed and we departed at 5.55 over the Blubberhouse Moors to Park Rash, our first observed hill.

Daybreak

By then it was light, but Jupiter was inclined towards feeling sad, using a fine drizzle as the outward and visible sign of his grief. It felt good on the face, but was definitely bad for the goggles, and we felt grateful for the lovely weather we had had during the night. A check at Kettlewell, about a mile before Park Rash, kept us waiting over 15 minutes, whereupon George suddenly decided his coat did not fit him and expected me to find a pin. Glad he did, for I found a suitable supplier in the form of a charming damsel appertaining to the local pub!

The S.S. 100 simply laughed Park Rash to scorn. So did all the other sidecars, but ours seemed to go up like the proverbial rocket with stones flying from the back wheel and enough power to slide the left-hand corner! Why must people fill in all the bad patches with tarmac? A week or so before the trial there was a real rough stretch here, but for fear of hurting the motorcars the road menders had done some all-too-efficient patching!

An uneventful, but delightful, journey brought us to Summer Lodge. The observed section through the S bends was easy, and farther up the hill the restart (three seconds were allowed, after stopping astride a line, to cross it with the back wheel) was not so easy but, nevertheless, within the capabilities of the machine in question, not forgetting the rider.

Up to now we had proceeded gently, but whether George was excited by the thought of refreshment in Brough or the bright sunshine I don't know; whatever the reason the result was one of the most exciting passages I have ever enjoyed. The big Brough Superior roared its way over the moors passing all traffic, except one gent. whose desire to be in front nearly overcame his natural dislike for bodily injury!

H. L. Takes Over

A salmon lunch at the County and Station Hotel, Carlisle, a glorious ride through the afternoon, which included three observed sections and a second stop and restart hill on the outskirts of Edinburgh, led us to the finishing check, where George finished his 28th London to Edinburgh trial and was able to claim his 26th Premier Award!

It was now my turn to do some work. The Pressman had to be at Donington by Sunday evening, so we removed our numbers, pointed the S.S. 100 towards Moffat, and away we went. Sitting in the chair was grand, but riding this super outfit was the "cat's whiskers," particularly with the maker himself "in the box." He did not seem unduly worried cruising along at 65-70

George Brough in the saddle and Henry Laird in the sidecar on their way to Edinburgh.

m.p.h., even when we had cause to show a large American car the way to hasten towards the Crook Inn. A nice place this. where they dispensed some very invigorating concoction called "Wee Willie Wassels" before we departed at 7.30 p.m. for Moffat.

The next morning we delayed our start until 8.45. However, once away, a comfortable cruising speed of 60-65 soon found us putting over 50 miles into the hour with the greatest of ease, and after leaving Catterick we covered the 20 miles into Boroughbridge in 20 minutes, 48 seconds. It is a good road, but it needs something better than merely a good machine to keep up a steady 70 m.p.h. without the slightest sign of distress. The handling, comfort,

brakes and general feel of the model, combined with the performance, all tend to make me appear unduly enthusiastic.

This is not by any means a routine test, but having arrived at Donington on Sunday evening I asked George if I might take the outfit away for a few days and test it for general performance against a stop-watch.

The maximum speed reached was 81 m.p.h., whilst the best timed run was 78.95 m.p.h. with a mean of two runs in each direction of 76.8 m.p.h. In the gears, the maximum speeds were equally impressive, namely 76 m.p.h. in third and 61 m.p.h. in second. At the bottom end of the scale the S.S.100 would trickle along at 8 m.p.h. in top, 5-6 m.p.h. in third and a slow walking pace in

second. The speedometer was checked and all the results were obtained with a passenger.

It took only 18 3/10 secs. to cover a standing quarter mile, the speed at the end being 73 m.p.h. The brakes brought the machine to rest in 41 ft. from 30 m.p.h., and the "all-in" fuel and oil consumptions were 43 m.p.g. and 4,000 m.p.g. respectively. Remarkable figures when the high average speeds are borne in mind.

The S.S.100 and sidecar form a combination which an enthusiast cannot help enthusing about, and any such person with £181 0s. 0d. to spend is able to have an identical outfit. If any purchaser enjoys his B.S. riding as much as I did that week-end, it won't be the last job he has from the Haydn Road works!

GEORGE BROUGH

Designer-Manufacturer-Rider of the Brough Superior, who has won over 200 Cups and Gold Medals in Open Competitions, Hill Climbs and Races in all parts of the World

As in the past, I propose to devote this first page of the Brough Superior catalogue to blowing my own trumpet, or, rather, the several trumpets of all who devote themselves to building "The Rolls-Royce of Motor Cycles" (*vide* "The Motor Cycle").

If this lack of modesty offends you, let me say that at one time we tried—really quite hard—to be modest. It couldn't be done. The lads who bought and rode my bikes systematically set about giving us swollen heads. Whenever we lay our trumpets down for a spell, B.S. enthusiasts take them up and blow themselves hoarse. See page 12 if you'd care to face *their* music . . .

Modesty is all very well up to a point, but one mustn't lose a sense of realities. If I, after twenty-seven years as Designer-Manufacturer-Rider, couldn't offer you something pretty exceptional in the way of fast, luxury motor cycles, the time would obviously have come for me to study the "Situations Vacant" column. You see, nobody on earth has been designing *and* manufacturing *and* riding bikes as long as yours truly, G.B. Experentia docet, and all that.

A year ago the S.S. 100 and 11.50 Brough Superiors were brought bang up to date by the standardisation of a rear springing system which is still unrivalled for neat appearance, lack of lateral motion, and sheer armchair riding comfort. The S.S.80 Special, specially launched to make B.S. ownership possible for hundreds who formerly could only heave covetous sighs, is the sole member of the "Brufsup" family without rear springing.

During the past twelve months I have racked my brains in vain for some way of producing finer twin-cylinder motor cycles than the S.S.100, S.S.80 and 11.50. Press critics and ordinary riders alike have been unable to find fault with those three lusty motors ; therefore they stand unchanged for 1939.

The newcomer to my range deserves and gets special literature to itself, although the preliminary introduction to the super-machine, by which this year's Show will long be remembered, will be found on pages 8 and 9. Here at last is the answer to the prayer of those fastidious idealists whose prose never ceases to adorn the "Dear Sir" pages of the technical Press. Read about this amazing new Four in my separate folder.

And don't forget that in matters of after-sales service the men who "Brough it" are the pampered darlings of motorcycledom. As a customer of mine said the other day : "You know, George, I think I'd go on buying your bikes even if they were bad—it's such a pleasure to deal with you and your Haydn Road boys."

George Brough.

GEORGE BROUGH HAYDN ROAD NOTTINGHAM

Telephones : 65535/6 Nottingham   Telegrams and Cables : "Brufsup, Nottingham"

YES—you *would* like George, a big, bluff, hearty sort of bloke with a deep, rumbling voice, healthy appetite and an eager readiness to join in any fun that's going. You should see him dealing with a four-gallon tankard and filling his enormous pipes to the accompaniment of booming chuckles!

He simply oozes personality, so magnetic in its influence that you'll invariably find a knot of people standing around him, drawn by an irresistible urge to know all he can reveal. He's boastful, mark you, and hints of past conquests in affected modesty—but there's a wicked gleam or two as he tells the story. I've always found him a splendid worker, and the type who produces an enormous output without seeming to hurry or make silly mistakes. He's not strictly modern in his ideas, but few people hold that against him because, whatever may be said, he's *very* sound in his outlook.

Persona Grata !

I introduced him to my wife and she fell for him rather heavily, with the result that he spent a hectic week-end with us. We took him to a road race meeting and all the boys promptly accepted him as a fine fellow on the spot. We took him on a country jaunt the following day and the most surprising people would suddenly recognize George wherever we were stopped and many impromptu discussions opened up.

On one occasion a rather prosperous gentleman stepped from his Bentley in a crowded car park, spotted George, and hurried across with a smile of recognition. It appeared that one of George's family had lived with him years ago and he was anxious to enquire how the folks were keeping.

CHARLES MARKHAM

Thinks That—

Small boys found deep fascination in just gazing at him; filled with awe and wonder they would ask questions about his achievements, whilst George stood around with a smug expression.

I met George in Nottingham. He was standing next to a bulbous sidecar—startlingly, but attractively finished in cream with crimson upholstery, armrests and "what-have-you." It was a Blacknell "Bullet" chariot and George appeared deeply attached to it. Being deep in conversation with Royal Enfield 125 c.c. expert E. O. Blacknell at the time, I suggested that "Blackie" might introduce me to this hefty bloke in the showroom.

The Last of the Line . . .

"Certainly," said, "Blackie," "I'd like you to meet him. Come right in and look at the last S.S. 100 Brough Superior—more's the pity, because it's a form of motor-cycling I rave about! Matchless 990 c.c. o.h.v. motor with hairpins, Castle forks and . . . well, you know a Brough without me pointing it all out!"

Following a five-minute gaze around I suggested that the S.S. 100 might appreciate an airing. In fact, I went further and hinted at a seven days' outing. "Blackie" stroked his chin thoughtfully, but promises to guard such desirable property were readily given and the Brough came with me on a 700-mile week.

"Don't forget," quoth George's guardian as we departed—"its *not* for sale, so don't you come back with a bundle of notes in lieu of!"

You know, of course, that every Brough answers to "George" and it's quite the accepted practice for other riders of the breed to give a cheery nod or a brief thumbs-up sign whenever and wherever encountered. Believe it or not, but I received and acknowledged such recognition four times in my first hundred miles—such is the depth of pride in possession retained by these big-twin enthusiasts.

A famous Brough owner was T. E. Lawrence— "Lawrence of Arabia"—who invariably christened successive mounts "George the First," "George the Second" and so on. Therefore, in naming this final member of the select family I felt I was merely upholding a fine tradition and that the Brough itself would doubtless appreciate the compliment

"YOU'D

LIKE

I consider it a matter for regret that so few riders have had the opportunity of sampling a "thousand twin." The fascination of riding and driving such a motor is not to be compared with any other type of engine unit, because it possesses a completely individual charm. To have experience of the lusty power available throughout the throttle range is to appreciate the feelings of those who swear by this type.

Turn back the grip and pobble at 15-18 m.p.h. in top with a laden sidecar—then, with a broad stretch of arterial beckoning m.p.h. without end, simply wind it up, and a seemingly unlimited number of healthy, thoroughbred horses arrive without complaint, fuss, or delay.

Essence of Brough

George possessed thin grips, a close-ratio four-speed box, and a degree of handling in harness so essentially Brough in effortless response—all of which meant averages well beyond average. "Cog-swapping" and grip-turning in the approved manner would provide progress so zestful as to make small sports-car drivers blink hard at George's rear plate. Long, swinging left-handers became "top of the bill" items even with the Blacknell chariot in "vacant and desirable possession" with "ev. mod. conv." trim.

With the speedometer hovering on "60 per" and the white centre line nearly hugged on the approach, it was sheer joy to sweep down the camber, clip the kerb close, and pull round with a smooth flow of b.h.p. as the chair visibly lightened its road contact. That right grip contained a full bundle of reassurance when twisting highways coincided with a need for fast travel, and many a soloist must have pondered in the wake of George's muted bass.

Should a main-road rise bring its usual gaggle of small saloons struggling valiantly to overcome the forces of gravity George would politely await an opening and the opportunity to soar majestically past whilst his twin fishtails burbled a song of seventy in third, with mellifluent resonance.

This is hardly a road test, but, if you like figures, I can tell you that George boasts a maximum, with bulbous appendage, of near enough to 82-83 m.p.h., what time I peep shyly to the off side of his steering-damper knob—an item of equipment used only for peeping around, because I never laid a fingerprint upon it. And I'm no Eric Oliver!

Despite unkind remarks from various clubmen pals that a bucket might serve better than a modest float chamber, I can vouch for the fact that, in his present single carburetter

The Last Member of a Famous Family Spends a Few Days as the Guest of "Motor Cycling"

". . . with a broad stretch of arterial beckoning m.p.h. without end, simply wind it up and a seemingly unlimited number of thoroughbred horses arrive without complaint, fuss or delay.

trim George cavorts, gallops, or meanders 55 miles to a gallon of Pool. Push him around with whip and spur and you produce a bare 50 m.p.g. Once you get to know him, you can rouse him with a single hefty swing of the starter, but I never cared to try it with a full ration of advance! A shade more "bite" on the front anchor would help to restrain his high spirits, although I cannot recall any tight moments during our brief friendship.

GEORGE!"

Reverting to this business of fine-line steering, I can instance occasions when George covered a mile in 60 seconds whilst I retained control with three fingers on the right grip only—and the passenger remained outwardly calm. As a matter of sober fact, photographer Long occupied the chariot

from Weedon to Willoughby one fine day, and I doubt if he even noticed the feat, being too busy watching curves come and go. That is sidecar navigation as it *should* be, but all too seldom is!

George was, of course, an expensive customer and in his pre-war days was regarded as the Rolls-Royce type. He represented the ultimate ambition of every "dyed in the wool" enthusiast, and, if I may judge by the number of tempting offers submitted to me as his temporary guardian, he *still* represents an ideal, irresistible even if unobtainable. Scores of people asked me if George's appearance in my company meant that his people were returning to our select circle. George himself was mute on the point, but I had to venture an opinion that there wasn't a hope in present circumstances. A sorrowful thought!

A Pennine Night

It was during a nocturnal journey over the Pennines in the velvety air of a true summer evening that I found George most co-operative. With his huge head lamp parting the curtain of darkness, he chuckled deeply at the steepening moorland roads and boomed with pleasure as he breathed loudly the refreshing air a thousand feet above sea level. Not for him the wheezing complaint at a seemingly endless climb—he just filled his big lungs and hustled his way upwards.

With the summit attained and twist-grip snapped shut, his fishtails emitted an occasional sharp hiccough, accompanied by stabs of flickering light, whilst we rushed into the distant valley. Yet one could forgive this obvious intoxication in remembering how often his family name has appeared in the lists of world records—and if George wants a little celebration now and then, who can blame him? After all, as the final member of an illustrous line he is a proud aristocrat to be regarded with due reverence.

You will see many of his direct antecedents on the roads of this and other countries. They all receive the amount of "pooh-jah" that their caste demands and hardly ever do you find one that has not had loving care lavished on it for most of its life. Sometimes, too, you see an example of one of George's more remote forebears—a stately old grandee still able to show the younger generation a thing or three. The cult of the "Bruff-Sup" is not merely a hankering after class distinction—it is true appreciation of something striving to be "a little better than the best."

To us all, George represents an ideal—the best obtainable for hard-earned cash—and although he may still be subject to criticism, human nature is such that exclusive possessions will always bring pride—and George is nothing if not exclusive, which is why I repeat, "You'd *like* George!"

". . . the last S.S. 100 Brough Superior—more's the pity . . . Matchless 990 c.c. o.h.v. motor with hairpins, Castle forks, and . . . well, you know a Brough . . !"

All-rounder No. 1

By "CASTOR"

Believe it or not, George was only 14 years old when photographed on this 1902 model, the first "all-Brough" production.

BEFORE, or in case, this "greatest-all-rounder" question develops into an unseemly brawl of words—see letter to the Editor in July 12 issue—your strongly biased correspondent would like, and hereby takes, the opportunity of throwing his weight into the scales in endorsement of "M.D.s" choice of all-time champ., viz., George Brough. It was he—your correspondent—who one day in '23 pranged a massive Welsh schoolfellow on the lug for suggesting that some obscure Celtic competitionist ranked above G.B. for the all-rounder stakes, and having sustained a fearful mauling on that occasion it is to be hoped that the pen will now prove mightier than the left-hook.

In writing of George one has to avoid the phrase "in his day," because his day is still here. The second of the two world wars has merely punctuated, not terminated, his career. At fifty-three, thirty-nine years after his first motorcycle trial, the Basford Bahnstormer still has an itching grip-wrist: it wouldn't be true to say, as they *do* say in all the best biographies, that he "never looks back," but he certainly does a lot more looking forward.

A Proud Record

In that part of his day that he's already had, let us say, then, George has probably won more high awards in long-distance trials than any man living or dead, ridden in the T.T. (once only, I grant you, and that without distinction), raced with success at Brooklands, held the "World's Fastest" title, won numerous sand events, and made a veritable corner in speed-trial and hill-climb fastest times.

The reader can think what he likes about the claims of other famous riders, including those listed by "M.D.," to the All-rounder No. 1 title. *Chacun*, as the French say, *á son goût*. George Dance, of course, was a virtuoso of the road circuits, a sprinter *par excellence* and a wizard of the half-day trial technique. Stanley Woods, aside from his amazing T.T. and Grand Prix sequence of supremacy, was ever a hard 'un to beat in the tougher type of trial and scramble.

In racing, the late Eric Fernihough

(Above) George all set for the End-to-End affair on his single-geared 2½ h.p. Brough on which many miles were of the pedal-assisted variety. Note the rigid front forks and the then fashionable peak - at - the - back cap!

(Right) Taken in 1923, this picture shows George on "Old Bill," the famous side-valve Brough Superior on which he obtained 51 Fastest Times of the Day in 52 open events.

on grass, and in almost every other field a rider of signal versatility.

The validity of George Brough's top placing partly depends on whether longevity of experthood be taken into account. Personally, I think it should be. Of course, the worst of these professional Peter Pans is that they make you feel so ancient. Despite the fact that when George made his competition debut your correspondent was a mere dottle of fertilizer down the bottom of the garden, I never talk to him without feeling that *I* am the Tired Business Man of the piece and he the up-and-coming grip-trouncer.

How did it all start, this remarkable and evergreen career of silverware snaffling? Well, it was "all over my jealous-ee," as the crooner hath it. George's elder brother, in the year 1906, had been entered by Brough, Sen., maker of the Brough motorcycle, for the A.C.C. Land's End-to-John o'Groats Trial. George, to use a phrase that was then practically in its infancy, "Took a Poor View" of staying home while his brother flashed forth upon this high adventure, and tore his sire off such a strip as seldom was heard in that inhibited epoch. Mr. Brough relented—George, after all, was something of a veteran already, having been fined six years earlier on a double rap of speeding and riding without a licence—and fitted out his Eton-collared progeny with a 2½ h.p. single-geared Brough for the End-to-End.

They called it a "Six Days" officially, but for George it took nine—after hundreds of miles of pedal-

ranged the whole gamut from 100 b.h.p. blown "thousands" to egg-cup one-seven-fivers; and I remember him once saying either that an M.C.C. triple Award *was* his most treasured possession, or that it would be if he had one—can't be sure now. As to Jock West, I would describe him as being not far short of the front rank in road racing, plumb *in* the front rank

assisted progress following the ill-timed demise of all but the odd half-horse on the way to the start.

The next season George burst into the racing game in a modest way with a series of smacks at local speed events, both uphill and on the level, a year later becoming an M.C.C. member and embarking on a career of long-distance trials that for sheer monotonous con-

George Brough, Collector of Silverware: a Haphazard Biographical Note

sistency of success has few parallels in motorcycle history. Those were the days when it was the privilege and pleasure of trials organizers to mortify the flesh of competitors in a big way. The "Edinburgh" trial took you (if you were lucky, muscular and resourceful) not merely *to* Edinburgh, but also back to London again afterwards, with a respite of only 30 hours in the Caledonian capital, stern and wild.

The destiny of the M.C.C. Challenge Cup, most coveted of all "Edinburgh" guerdons, depended almost entirely on split-second timekeeping. After winning the cup twice in a row in '10 and '11, George was right on his mettle in 1912 to make it a permanent item of

(Above) In 1922 George made his first appearance at Brooklands on "Spit and Polish." He won the 5-lap Experts' Scratch Race and the model was the first side-valver to lap the track at 100 m.p.h.

(Left) In 1928 George tore down the Arpajon straight at 130.6 m.p.h. on this monster to achieve the "fastest ever" one-way speed at that date.

get him if he didn't watch out. Well, he didn't and it did, as history records in many of her ampler pages. It is not every 1940 machine that would repeat that 1912 does of the old Broughs, over roads of 1912 quality. Those old 'uns—the best of them, anyway—had something. They had light weight for their power, and their silky belt drive absorbed the rough chunks of engine prang.

George's "Edinburgh" reminiscences, told with that jerky trick of speech he has, as though he were perpetually on the brink of a verbal misfire, are never-ending and full of great gusty laughs. He remembers, for instance, when Charles Needham, that hard-riding Brummell of the highway, all-white breeches a n d sumptuous raiment, was purging into Penrith at a sharp trot when away across his bows sauntered a ruminating citizen with a

the Brough home bric-á-brac. Once more and it would be his to have and to hold. . . .

At Doncaster, on the outward trip, the officials convened an Extraordinary General Huddle to break the news to George, Harold Karslake and Frank Smith that they were within seconds of each other for the cup. A total of 70 checks were taken on the north-bound run. Coming back, checks aggregated 74. For good measure they started taking them from ambush between milestones, as well as *at* milestones. For hour after spine-jolting hour the Big Three rode with one hand clutching a throttle lever and the other a stop-watch. At the finish George was announced as the winner with an error of less than 10 seconds in 24 hours!

That, he says, was the toughest job of his whole riding career. "Per ardua ad Edinburgh." For hours after the finish he teetered around in a mile-tipsy daze, nerve-numbed victim of a sort of organic pre-ignition. But the pot had come to stay. . . .

With 23 premier awards among his Edinburgh souvenirs—he has competed 24 times in the M.C.C. Whitsun classic—George Brough regards Scot-

(Right) Still quite a young lad! George snapped during "Motor Cycling's" 1939 Donington Day aboard his favourite SS 100 model. Sorry we cannot include a picture of him on the latest Brough Superior, but we hope to do so shortly!

land as a happy hunting ground. It was in 1912 that he ran through the Scottish Six Days on a 6 h.p. *single-geared* Brough with all toolbags sealed, tacking an extra 20 miles on to the official course distance to make up a round thousand. For all normal going during the trial the Brough pulled a $3\frac{7}{8}$ to 1 gear, this being dropped to $4\frac{1}{2}$ to 1 (by fitting a belt of different section) for "pieces of resistance" like Amulree, Applecross and Kenmore.

The big-twin bug would

rapt expression and not a care in the world. Needham stabbed the horn button, bellowed like a pole-axed bison, braked, slid, tore a great widening black weal in the sun-softened tarmac, came down *WHAM*, fouled his faultless breeches beyond recognition, opened his mouth to rain contumelies on the heedless jay—and discovered in the nick of time that said jay was stone deaf and plumb dumb!

The *Cirque de Brough* is an event you will never find slated in the international calendar. Open by invitation to the Bruffsupping *elite* only, it has, in the course of years, attained a certain limited celebrity as a fits-and-starts progress from the finish of the " Edinburgh " back to Nottingham, by way of almost anywhere except Mull, Eigg and Rum, those alcoholic-sounding western isles. Many and varied are the stories told of the *Cirque de Brough*, though neither so many nor so varied as those that aren't and can't be told.

Karslake's Catastrophe

George minds the time when the *Cirque de Brough* brotherhood, headed south after an " Edinburgh," came across gaunt and harassed Harold Karslake a-halt at the roadside investigating what he described as a " click in the front wheel " of his gigantic Karbro Express. This phenomenon the volubly derisive Bruffsuppers diagnosed as a dropped-in exhaust valve—which it was. So what do they do? They remove the offending 750 c.c. pot, hoik out the debris and reassemble to a most exacting " drill " intoned by the anxiously watchful owner. They know, but he doesn't, that when the gudgeon pin is poked back in (" Steady there . . . hold it . . . for pity's sake, steady . . . up a fraction . . . *now* push! ") it goes *over* instead of through the con.-rod.

So, after four hours reassembling time, there is *still* that aggravating " click in the front wheel " !

Then there was the Strange Case of the Big Stiff, a Broughian recollection of the 1912 Exeter Run.

In company with two other riders of single-geared Broughs, George had been plugging away for hours through blinding rain. Drenched, fed up and far from home, the trio presently chuffed to a standstill somewhere on Salisbury Plain to see what could be done about chronic belt-slip. Through the blackness they could just make out the silhouette of a shed. Diving within for shelter, the Basford Bahnstormer lit a match and swooped delightedly upon a nice, dry-looking sheet which lay spread out over an amorphous lump of nothing in particular in a corner of the building.

The amorphous lump proved to be a rather well-knit corpse, which leered up balefully at the intruders. Where all the best old-fashioned remedies might have failed, sheer power of fright effected a cure for belt-slip in that awesome moment!

When you start writing of George's racing career, it's hard to avoid becoming a mere catalogue-compiler. And if you aren't careful, particularly if he has any say in the matter, you find yourself ricochetting off at a tangent into the careers of the likes of Ron Storey, Arthur Greenwood, Ted Baragwanath, Eric Fernihough, Fred Dixon, Tommy Spann, George Patchett, Joe Wright, and all the rest of those B.S.-tamers who have nuzzled famous chins into the tank-shops of history-making Bruffsups.

A pridefully remembered quick-change act by a B.S. stands out in the 1929 chronicle of the marque. A fortnight after George had won his customary " Edinburgh " premier, the same basically standard SS.100, with a racing mag. substituted for the Mag-dyno, a larger carburetter and some of the road-going furniture jettisoned, ripped over the Saltburn kilometre in Ron Storey's hands at 122.9 m.p.h. That was Britain's " fastest ever " on sand—and still is. The heads had not even been removed since finishing the " Edinburgh."

On the sprint front, after graduating by successive stages from his famous " Old Bill " side-valve, which in the

1922-23 era had trousered him 51 firsts out of 52 consecutive events, the climax of George's personal career as a dicer came with the attainment of 130.6 m.p.h. one way of the Arpajon stretch in '28. That was the highest speed ever officially clocked on a motorcycle to that date, although the failure of the specially built SS.100 to make the return trip intact (" One piston," George recalls, *would* try to go up the wrong cylinder ") ruled it out as a world's record.

Gold Star Grief

The only sidecar outfits to lap Brooklands at over a hundred have all been Brough Superiors. George's effort to qualify for a " chair " Gold Star, although unavailing, he remembers as one of the most morale-shaking events in all his years as a dicer. The outfit, comprising an ordinary road-going chair, a standard 1927 frame and a 1933 " two-of-everything " engine, could scarcely have been worse suited to the permanent waves of the old Saucer: in no wise could it be compared with the specialist track hardware used by " Barry " and Fred Dixon for their successful Gold Star sorties.

For perhaps a third of that hell-raising lap two or more wheels were pawing the air. When, as occasionally happened, all three treads touched down simultaneously, the outfit pointed itself first at Oxshott, next at Bagshot, then in turn at all those other townships immortalized by the poet—anywhere, in fact, except the way it was meant to go. Those involuntary meanderings cost George 0.79 m.p.h. and the coveted Star. Those were moments; yes, sir!

Well, " M.D.," if by any chance you should ever meet up with a certain freckle-panned Welshman and he should tell you that an unpronounceable Celt, of whom you've never heard, is Britain's No. 1 All-rounder, agree with him before he knocks you senseless. In all other circumstances do as I do and go on rooting for George!

HE's AFTER THE DOUBLE CENTURY!

Noel Pope Sails Next Week with his Brough-Superior for a "World's Fastest" Bid on Bonneville Flats

A T last the lid is lifted from a secret that has been kept under boiling pressure for over six months and "Motor Cycling" is able to give the first fully illustrated description of the big blown Brough-Superior on which Noel Pope will attack the World's Motorcycle Speed Record next month.

This week a small party of "in-the-know" people, who have watched the development of this audacious venture, have been celebrating the conclusion of the final tests, christening the glittering, streamlined monster in the traditional fashion and generally extending good wishes and "happy voyage" to the rider and his associates, who set out on August 13 on the "Queen Elizabeth" for New York, with Salt Lake City and the Bonneville Flats of Utah as their destination.

Planning

And so comes the last stage but one in the fulfilment of a dream that has been Noel Pope's for over ten years—to regain for Britain the World's Fastest title, held since 1937 by the German high-speed ace, Ernst Henne, on a supercharged 494 c.c. B.M.W. at 174 m.p.h. Through the war years Pope never ceased to cogitate on the project. He knew exactly what he wanted to do. His plan was to rebuild his famous 996 c.c. Brough-Superior, with which he set up the all-time Brooklands solo and sidecar lap records (125 and 107 m.p.h. respectively), and to equip it with a body shell as near aerodynamically perfect as possible. He was confident that he had the right idea and, when he came out of the Army, he made tentative efforts to put the work in hand. He soon found, however, that 1946 was not a propitious year for ventures of this sort. The financial difficulties, exchange control problems and so forth appeared insuperable and he reluctantly shelved his dream.

But suddenly hope dawned again. His employer, Teddy Comerford, turned up at their Thames Ditton premises one day last February and said, in effect, "Look, Noel, I know your heart is set on this record business. Like the boy in the soap advertisement, you won't be happy till you get it. O.K., then, go ahead and I'll look after the cost."

Co-operation

And Ted had no need to say it twice. Noel had brushed the cobwebs off the staunch old Brough and was at work on it that very same day. The telephone wires to Nottingham and Tottenham sang with the glad tidings. George Brough and Teddy Prestwich were "in" on the job like a flash, George to overhaul the machine, J.A.P.s to overhaul the engine. Following the line set by their founder, Lord Wakefield, who was always ready to help with record activities, the "Castrol" people offered their valuable aid and "Dickie" Davies, of Dunlops, got weaving on the not inconsiderable problem of tyres to resist the high speeds envisaged.

Pope's plan was to use his veteran war horse almost exactly as it was

(Above) Noel Pope. (Right) Made to measure. The supporting members of the light alloy shell in position on the Brough-Superior.

(Below) The stabilizing fin and the tail member nearing completion. Below the gearbox can be seen the retractable balancing wheels.

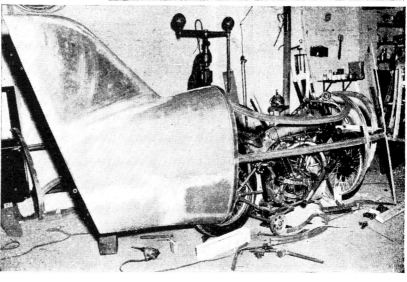

Coupled to a dynamometer, the 1,000 c.c. J.A.P. engine recorded sufficient power to beat the record by a handsome margin.

The 1/3rd scale wooden model undergoing wind tunnel tests which decided the final form of the shell.

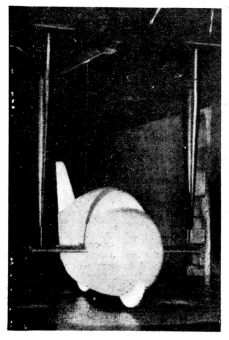

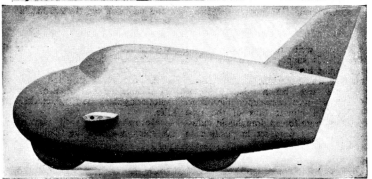

The test model shows to advantage the scientific streamline shape of the shell. A Perspex-fronted hinged roof will be fitted to the machine.

originally built for the Brooklands records, but to renew certain engine parts and enclose the whole in a streamlined shell. He retained the Powerplus supercharger, mounted forward of the engine, and all such fittings as Castle forks, tank, brakes, three-speed gearbox, handlebars, saddle mounting and so forth were unaltered. The engine has had a new crankcase and cylinder barrels, but the heads, with coil valve springs and balanced rockers, are the original ones used before the war.

Scientific Design

The Pope design for a body shell was submitted to Blackburn and General Aircraft, Ltd., at Brough, Yorks, who, from his references, made up a 1/3rd scale model in wood, which was submitted to most exhaustive and lengthy wind-tunnel tests. These were made in order to determine the drag and general aerodynamic stability of the model, which, as will be seen from the photographs, provides full enclosure for the rider and has a rear fin and a pair of "stub wings," or aerofoils, located some 16 ins. aft of the front wheel centre line. These wings, which have their leading edges canted downwards, are intended to press the machine onto the ground at high speed, and the fin is, of course, to improve lateral stability.

The results of the tests can be briefly expressed in the Blackburn company's own summary. "It is suggested that the aerofoil could be reduced consider-

ably in size, and it may be possible to dispense with it altogether, since the body itself, in the presence of the ground, develops a negative lift. The body alone is directionally unstable and the addition of the fin makes the combination neutrally stable or, possibly, just stable. It is considered that the fin is essential.

"The wind-tunnel measurement is in substantial agreement with that given in ref. 1 [one of N. B. Pope's own estimations], resulting in a gross drag coefficient of 0.00024, compared with the estimated value of 0.00026. This should result in a maximum speed based on the power output and tractive resistance given in ref. 1 of 307 ft. per sec. (209 m.p.h.) at sea level."

More Figures

It was carefully pointed out, of course, by the Aerodynamics Laboratory that these results were obtained with a smooth-surfaced model and that no allowance had been made for the apertures for wheels, exhaust pipes, and so on—but that estimate of 209 m.p.h. was good enough for Noel. It confirmed his designs, and what particularly pleased him was the discovery that, even without the stub wings, the

natural tendency of the machine would be to stick to the ground with an ever-increasing hold as the speed mounted. Indeed, the wheel loadings, without the stubs, at 204 m.p.h. worked out at −130 lb. on the front and −22.5 lb. on the rear.

Work on the shell was therefore put in hand and a panel-beating expert, Mr. G. Tidey, of Wimbledon, set about producing the components from extruded-section frame members and sheet aluminium.

Bench Tests

Three weeks ago J.A.P.s finished work on the engine, but they had no dynamometer capable of dealing with the horse-power anticipated. This set Noel a small problem: other water brakes that he investigated either worked up to only 100 b.h.p. or were big machines coping with several hundred horse-power. At length he ran to earth a brand-new Heenan and Froude installation set up in the workshop of Mr. Lucas, not far from Chessington Zoo. Mr. Lucas is an automobile experimental engineer and was formerly associated with Mr. Harry Weslake, whose prowess as a turner

Close-up of the power unit undergoing bench tests. This engine holds the Brooklands Lap Record at 125 m.p.h. and may well top the 200 m.p.h. mark on the Salt Lake.

will be well remembered by all Brooklands supporters. It was when the engine had been fitted in the frame and the whole machine securely bolted to the test bench that "Motor Cycling's" men came upon the scene.

Powerful blower fans of the type used to create forced draughts in industrial furnaces were set in position to send a cooling air stream over the cylinders and a special coupling connecting engine shaft with the water brake was given its final check-over. Then came the great moment. From a spluttering start, the J.A.P. crackled into life.

Meanwhile, the shell was nearing completion. Also the "landing gear"

had been proved satisfactory. This consists of a pair of wheels mounted on the extremities of spring-loaded legs bolted to the saddle- and chain-stays on each side of the machine. A Bowden control from the handlebars enables Pope to lift his "undercarriage" at the flick of a lever.

Secret Venue

The venue of the test run, when the machine, body and man finally came together, must remain a secret, but when it was completed Noel was able to emerge from his shell and report to his sponsors that he was ready to keep his date with the "Queen Elizabeth."

Next week he, George Brough, Ted Comerford and the "Brufsup" set out on the last stage of the great experiment. On reaching American shores they will be met and chaperoned by Mr. George Eyston, one of Wakefields' directors and a man whose vast experience of high-speed record breaking will be an invaluable asset to the venture.

And what a venture it is! Few, except those who have seen the "back-room" work, can appreciate the enormous amount of effort, skill and brain that has been put into the project by this little band of sportsmen. And now that stage one has been completed there looms ahead the crucial second phase. In the brief duration of a few seconds it will be seen whether the labours of six intense months bring in their train the highest prize a motorcyclist can win. Until we know the answer we can say no more than "bon voyage and the very best of luck!"

Brough Superior 11-50 SPECIAL

Completely equipped with Fully Sprung Rear Wheel, Special Lucas Magdyno Lighting Set, Altette Horn, Rear Wheel Driven Speedometer with illuminated dial, Rolling Stand, Pillion Footrests and "Fort" Tyres,

All component parts fitted to Brough Superior machines are made exclusively to my designs and special requirements.

"At Brooklands track, Pope, Noel of the ilk, mounted and flew . . ."

Who's Afraid of—

The Big Blown Brough?

Highlights in the Career of NOEL POPE, One of the Bravest Men on Wheels

By DENNIS MAY

"LEND me your wings! I mount! I fly!" carolled Alexander Pope, most quotable of English poets, in the year 1739. At Brooklands track, one damp afternoon just 200 years later, another Pope, Noel of the ilk, mounted and flew; flew as no rider had ever flown around that hallowed bowl before, or ever will again, had we only known it. But he sensibly forebore to call on anyone for the loan of their wings. Experience had taught Noel that chaps weren't interested in lending other chaps anything—much less paying out good money—to enable them to break the Brooklands lap record, a feat, perhaps, without equal as a test of courage, skill and strength.

Time was when the record had been worth quite a stack. Joe Wright, for example, when he came to add up the score after turning the track at 118.86 m.p.h. on a Zenith-J.A.P. in 1929, found himself better off by about £200 in bonuses. Then, in 1935, Pope raised it to 120.59 on the ex-Baragwanath, supercharged Brough Superior, and the late Eric Fernihough, Broughing *sans compressor*, answered with 123.58 m.p.h. a few weeks later, suffering chastisement where it hurts most, when his rear tyre tread peeled as the B.-S. crossed the line.

Learning that the bonus barons proposed rewarding their efforts with a fiver, Eric and Noel ganged up and called a truce, *sine die*. For them, the record could henceforth stay where it stood. It wasn't so much the principle of the thing as the money.

Came the summer of '39. The lap record was still where Ferni had put it. Eric, poor fellow, was dead—killed at Gyon, Hungary, in his last attempt to take the world's maximum mark away from Henne, B.M.W., and Germany. That left Pope as the sole prospective candidate for the track record. War, he felt sure, was just around the corner. This certainty bestirred him to a final assault. The bonus dispensers couldn't care less about the matter, but now, for Noel, it was the principle of the thing and not the money.

For a start, everything went wrong. Either the Brough wouldn't play and the weather would or vice versa, by turns, with the occasional variant of neither playing.

It wasn't raining at Brooklands on July 4, 1939, but it had been. There were patches of water on the concrete. Also, a blustery wind was blowing. The Brough, on the other hand, was firing to the queen's taste. Something told Noel, as he conned a cloud-blotched sky, that it was now or never. Well, O.K., make it now. The timekeeper stopped tapping an impatient toe and put his clocks through a precautionary stop and restart. Pope did a couple of warming laps, came in, changed plugs, then set off on the un-timed lap that would give him flying speed. "I mount! I fly!"

It would take "Ixion's" gift for descriptive writing to do justice to that lap record to end all lap records, which is literally what it was; me, I think, I won't try. Eighty seconds flat was the time which, the way the speed tables told it, equalled 124.5 an hour. But the speed tables, of course, were based on a centre-line perimeter measurement, and Pope was way outside the centre-line from start to finish of that historic tour de brute force. Posterity will, therefore, have it that the Brooklands record stands for all

Pope on his supercharged Brough Superior-J.A.P. sans aluminium shell

time at 124½, but *we* know, don't we, that Pope must have gone round at, anyway, 127.

At that gallop the outer circuit has to be ridden like a road course. Taking a line close to the lip of both bankings, Noel had to use every ounce of his strength to warp the B.-S. over far enough to get round at all. Approaching Vickers' works, he was knocking sparks off the concrete with his left footrest. Leaving the Fork, the opposite peg gouged the ground. Over the timed kilometre

Front view of the "Silver Fish" which Pope took to Utah.

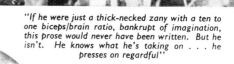

"If he were just a thick-necked zany with a ten to one biceps/brain ratio, bankrupt of imagination, this prose would never have been written. But he isn't. He knows what he's taking on . . . he presses on regardful"

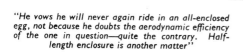

"He vows he will never again ride in an all-enclosed egg, not because he doubts the aerodynamic efficiency of the one in question—quite the contrary. Half-length enclosure is another matter"

Pope at Utah. Television preparations were being made when this picture was taken

on the Railway Straight he was making 145 m.p.h., and the highest rev-indicator reading along that straight matched 160 an hour.

When he pulled in and climbed off, his hands were shaking like a dipso's—uncontrollably.

I have often speculated on the comparative exhaustion factors of a record Brooklands lap, on the one hand, and the more rigorous forms of road racing, on the other. Noel has the key to such speculations, and an authoritative one, too, for back when many present-day T.T. and Manx riders were being kept up with safety pins, he was going the rounds of the Continental Circus. No road race, he says, ever knocked the forcemeat out of him the way a jiffysnipping track lap did on the Brough, or anywhere near it.

Who's afraid of the big blown Brough? There have, I think, been quite a few occasions when Noel Pope was. That's what I admire about him : if he were just a thick-necked zany with a ten to one biceps/brain ratio, bankrupt of imagination, this prose would never have been written. But he isn't. He knows what he is taking on, it scares him inside, he presses on regardful.

Whether Pope will one day return to the assault on the maximum record remains to be seen. He declines to commit himself. But here is as good a place as any to set down the full and authentic story of the ill-starred Comerford-Pope bid in 1949 on the Bonneville Salt Flats.

Eggless Tests

When, three weeks after the arrival of Ted Comerford, George Brough and Noel in the Utah wilderness, their hardware finally showed up from England, the machine itself but not its streamlined shell was forthwith uncrated and readied for test runs. The "egg", it was decided, could wait until after the Brough had proved itself *au point* mechanically. The eggless tests were duly carried out : geared for 200 m.p.h. at the peak of the power curve, the machine actually did 150, meaning that the aluminium and Perspex gazebo would need to stick on at least another 25 an hour when the time came, as it easily should by all the slipstick calculations.

Satisfied, Ted Comerford ordered the egg de-boxed, only to find that in course of shipment it had broken away from its moorings inside the crate and incurred a most severe case of cauliflower ear. Panel-beating experts restored the contours . . . but when our chaps came to marry up the three main sections of streamlining (on the model, that is) it was found that nothing met anything anywhere. Here was a beaut of a quandary, because the A.A.A. timekeepers had all reported for duty and, as I know from experience, an A.A.A. clock-clicking crew, although a lovesome thing, comes expensive (about £100 a day, all told, that far from civilization).

Taking a chance, Pope posted two big toughies at the north end of the Brough and two at the south end and exhorted them to push in opposite directions. When they had finished pushing the shell appeared to make some sort of sense, but not as much as the heart could wish for. However, Noel ran.

At about 150 miles an hour in second (correct, Reader Majoribanks, this bolide has a three-speed box), the Brough started angling very slightly off course to port. Normally that wouldn't have mattered much, because the world is a big place and the Flats are a big bit of the world. But for once it did matter ; during the party's three-weeks' wait for the arrival of the machine and stuff, posses of

local speed demons had been exercising their hot-rod cars over the chosen brine tracts, reducing the width of faultless straightaway to perhaps sixty feet. On each flank of that ribbon the salt was cut up into long, ugly ripples.

Realizing the certain consequences of trying to steer by the bars, Noel fought to edge 'er back on course by leaning. But the wind-tunnel boffins had been right—yes, indeed !—when they said their gazebo would give positive directional stability. Having assumed this new direction—due, of course, to the al fresco reblocking mentioned above—there was no talking her out of it.

When mere inches separated the Brough from the Moto-Cross terrain, Pope thought well, hell, you're only middle-aged once, let's have a go, and did. But it didn't surprise him that the response to his handlebar mauling was zero. A split-second later the Brough went into a lock-to-lock wobble. Pope fumbled frenziedly for the release catch on the inside of the roof, but before he could come to grips with it, the roof was torn off by natural causes and he personally was perabolating Daks over dandruff through the air.

Landing, he slid along the brine face upwards, a yard or two ahead of the Brough. His braces then broke and his breeches and jerkin were half torn off, exposing that which it is their business to conceal. Skating barebacked over searing salt at probably two miles a minute was not funny, but he hadn't time to register the thought before the bicycle caught up with him, simultaneously rearing end over end and coming down on top of him with a wham fit to dislodge yesterday's breakfast.

Machine Going Rogue

From Ditton, Surrey, to the Salt Desert, however, is a long way, and Pope, although feeling pretty redundant as a result of this misadventure, wasn't minded to head for home without a second try. But the egg was, henceforth, out. He vows he will never again ride in an all-enclosed egg, not because he doubts the aero-dynamic efficacy of the one in question—quite the contrary—but on the grounds that it simply scares him rigid to travel at those speeds in a metal galosh. Half-length enclosure—what might be termed a broken egg — is another matter. He wouldn't mind that at all.

He was, he admits, in too much of a hurry to get on with the final eggless run which, as he well knew, was anyway foredoomed to failure. In himself he had been very badly shaken and bruised, and such physical derangements are seldom without effect on a man's state of mind. Obviously, they had affected his. In the ordinary way, for he is a methodical, exacting subject by nature, he would never have straddled the B.-S. a second time without first going over it with a microscope and litmus paper. This time he didn't. He did check it, certainly, but not with his customary thoroughness.

A few days later, after nursing his bruises from deep purple through turquoise to mustard colour, but still in a state when he could only just sit a machine, he roared off once more down the black marker line. Speed : 146 m.p.h., which was about as good as anyone expected. Back at the make-do pits he reported that gears were jumping out and the whole machine was going rogue at speed. Something funny at the back end, he thought.

Correct. The frame was broken.

Pope working on the Brough before leaving for Utah. In the foreground is a ¼-scale model of the streamlined machine

The power beneath the throne. A close-up view of the lusty 1,000 c.c. Matchless engine

Broughing Down to Brighton

A Wintry Run to the Coast and Back with a Sidecar Outfit That Was Different—By JOHN MILLS

IF, in pre-war days, you ever became involved in an argument concerning the relative merits (or otherwise) of different makes of machine, you could end the discussion by saying, "Oh, yes, but you cannot beat the old Brough." Even the most enthusiastic owners of other models had to agree, and the subject could be changed without further argument. The Brough Superior had become more than a trade mark; it was almost a legend, and although there were thousands of riders who had never ridden a "Brufsup" they all agreed that it was the king of the lot.

I, personally, had never ridden a Brough or even sat on the saddle of one; so when my old friend Mike Harton, sales manager of George Grose, Ltd., rang me up one day and told me he had found a Brough S.S.100 with Black Alpine sidecar, and would I like a little ride round in it, you can imagine my reactions!

The Brough had come into Harton's hands in rather an unusual way. It was first bought in 1938, and the owner had covered some 20,000 miles when war broke out. He rode it into a lock-up garage, turned off the petrol, and joined the Forces. Thirteen years later he approached the owner of the garage, Eric Bowles, well-known Clapham motor engineer, and said in effect, "Look here, my wife does not fancy riding in the Brough any more, would you like to buy it?"

Eric bought the model like a flash and rang up Mike Harton to tell him about it. Together they went into the damp, dirty

Harton takes over the steering, while Mills tries to find some shelter behind the shattered windscreen

There is plenty of room in the Black Alpine sidecar even for the long legged Mike Harton

garage, seized a filth-covered sidecar outfit and hauled it out into the light. At first, they were not very impressed. Thirteen years in a garage with no attention does not improve a machine's appearance. Then Harton tentatively removed some of the dirt from the massive tank Untarnished chromium plating sparkled at him! Bowles and Harton got busy. They cleaned off as much of the dirt as possible on the spot and were quite amazed at what they saw. A genuine S.S.100 with Black Alpine chair in what amounted to showroom condition. The tyres were pumped up, and Harton flooded the carburettor—1939 petrol was still in the tank. At the third kick the mighty 1,000 c.c. overhead-valve Matchless twin engine burbled into life—just like that!

Bowles got to work in earnest with water and rags, changed the oil, fitted a new battery, and had a cautious ride round the block. The Brough burbled as happily as if it had spent only a week-end in the garage. Harton, in the meantime, was consumed with jealousy and demanded a gallop. "Have the thing for the week-end if you like," was the generous answer. Almost needless to say, this offer was seized upon.

When I first saw the Brough I was astonished. It seemed almost incredible that a machine could stand all that time with no attention and still look in the superb condition it did. The tank was entirely free from rust and the plating absolutely unmarked. Here and there on the wheels the enamel had been attacked, and there were a few other patches where the damp had worked in. The sidecar was very nearly 100 per cent perfect—only a few traces of very light rust marred the "funk-bar," and the screens had turned yellow with age. Somebody had put his fist through the windscreen, making a nice little hole near the top. When I commented on this, Harton turned rather red, so I forbore from making further remarks.

After we had finished looking at the thing, Harton suggested a run round the City. "Why not a run down to Brighton or somewhere?" he then asked. Why not, indeed? It was all fixed up in no time at all. On Sunday, Harton and the Brough would be at the Dorset House car park; I would put my solo in dock for the day and we would take it in turns to drive to Brighton and back. We decided not to venture farther afield in case the model developed any serious faults.

The day before the run was bitterly cold, and a few flakes of snow were falling in my part of the world. That evening it was still colder, and the met. people announced it would be fine and cold the next day. Sunday morning was a shocker. When I woke up I could see the bare branches of the trees outside covered with frost, the grass was a sheet of frozen snow, and the roads—oh, those roads! Glistening, scintillating ice flashed at me as the pale, watery sun leaked miserably through menacing snow clouds. Still, the die was cast—and off I went. Very slowly, I might add. I was taking no chances with my solo on a day like this.

Eventually I reached Dorset House and there was Harton, the Brough, and a shivering photographer waiting for me. Some pictures were taken and then Harton offered me the driver's seat. "No thanks," I replied, "I have not driven sidecars often enough to take this job through South London on a day like this. You pilot it for the first few miles." I hopped into the sidecar and we set off.

Now I have been driven in quite a number of sidecars down the Blackfriars Road, but never one like this. Southwark Borough Council, which is running an "Ancient Southwark" publicity campaign, has taken things a little too far by providing genuine Ancient Briton roads. As a rule, one gets a first-class shaking over the wavy, pot-holed cart track called Blackfriars Road. Not in the Alpine, though. Apart from a gentle quivering, we might have been on a super *autobahn*.

The machine was riding the bumps well. There were no signs that the driver was getting a battering from the frightful surface, even without rear-springing. It was very tricky that morning. The tram-tracks were glistening with ice, puddles had frozen over, and the wood blocks and cobbles had that horrible glazed sheen that, in solo circumstances, would have forced me miserably into the gutter for a spot of wheel-grip. The Brough sailed calmly over the surface with never a trace of waver or slide. The big vee-twin engine gurgled softly in my ear, the sidecar was delightfully warm and cosy, and I felt at peace with the world.

Eventually we cleared London. Harton said he would just wind her up for a bit and then I could take over. Past the de-restriction sign, down into second, and round with the grip!

John Mills meets the Brough for the first time, and finds that the 14-year-old chromium plating on the tank is still unblemished

The gentle murmur of the Matchless engine suddenly changed into a snarl, and the scenery blurred as the big Brough leaped forward. A flick of the wrist, a deeper note to the exhaust, and even more speed. Then, as Mike snapped into top, the damaged windscreen which had been bulging slightly for the last couple of miles suddenly gave up the struggle and burst into fragments. Pieces of celluloid whipped past my head, and an icy, breath-stopping gale roared through the shattered framework.

"Eighty !" yelled Harton, as a roundabout loomed up and the speed dropped off. We sailed round the roundabout, and on the other side we changed places.

The Brough has inverted levers for the brake and exhaust-lifter. As I went to engage first gear I took a firm handful of exhaust-lifter. The engine stopped. Muttering an oath, I dismounted and prepared for a battle with one thousand cubic centimetres. Nothing of the sort. Just ease the front piston over compression, a merest shade of throttle, half-retard, and a gentle push on the kick-starter brought the engine woffling back into life.

The riding position of the Brough was a little strange at first. One had to stretch out more than with a post-war machine, but in fact the position was very good. The clutch, which was as light as those on 197 c.c. two-strokes, took up the drive in the last half-inch of travel. The gear lever, although having a longer movement than those I prefer, fell readily to a bewadered foot, and the gears went in quietly and certainly.

Way You Do It

Now my own personal machine, a 650 c.c. twin, is a very potent performer, and I thought that the big engine under me would not be very much more powerful. I do not suppose it is, really, but, as Cab Calloway says, "It ain't what you do, it's the way that you do it." Instead of the revs sliding smoothly up the scale, the vee-twin burbled for a few yards then snarled with a savage ferocity as the power came on, and in no time at all the speedo needle was registering 30 m.p.h.

"Took off in second," I thought, but I hadn't. It was bottom gear all right, with the engine sounding quite leisurely at 30. A quick change into second and the Brough surged forward. Change again at 50—this vee-twin is amazing ! I was chuffing along at about 60 m.p.h. when I remembered that I could not drive a sidecar very well ! This outfit was driving itself. No tugging at the bar was necessary at all. Greatly daring, I lifted one hand from the handlebar and then the other. For a long way the Brough steered perfectly hands off and then, because of the camber, it began to veer toward the kerb and I steered out properly.

If ever there was a duo-personality machine, this was it. Use the throttle and gearbox properly and you had a super-sports model that would show its heels to many a 500 c.c. solo. On the other hand, it was possible to drop down to 25 m.p.h. in top gear and woffle away from this speed without snatch or fuss. The Brough had all the best points of a woolly side-valve and a hot o.h.v.

The run down to Brighton I usually regard as rather boring. Scenery is nothing to get excited about and the road is not exactly in the super class. On this cold winter's morning we had chosen

for the trip, the scenery was even more depressing. Stark, bare trees, leafless bushes, and frost-whitened grass are not very inspiring, and the sun was not able to force its way through the heavy mist that was settling down in places. At the Half Way Café we changed places again, and Harton put on his waders.

Mike is a sidecar exponent of the first water. Where I had been content with a modest 60 plus, he wanted to flatten the Brough. From my snug seat in the sidecar (by sitting to one side one could avoid the worst of the gale that tore through the shattered windscreen) I could hear the thunder of the exhaust as the engine began to churn out the power. Faster and faster we went as the miles were piled up. Eventually Harton screamed "Eighty-five !" and soon we flashed past the Pylons that mark the town limits.

In Brighton, we rumbled along at thirty in top and selected a café on the front at which to lunch. It was a terrible day on the coast : grey, damp and cold, with the crews of cars gazing dismally out of their windows at the sullen sea. The hardy spirits who had ventured out for a walk were shuffling past with their collars turned up and their hands thrust into their pockets, snuffling miserably at the biting wind that tore in from the sea.

We shuddered in sympathy and turned towards the café. Just as we were about to go in I noticed a very large policeman taking a car driver's details. I nudged Mike. "Surely they're not having a parking purge on Sunday," I whispered. If they were, our Brough would be next on the list. We were just about to nip smartly back to the machine when I noticed the unfortunate car driver still had a green flash on his Road Fund licence. What a nerve ! To park a car with last year's licence on Brighton sea-front ! Still, he won't do that again.

Flurry of Snow

We had a meal and then trundled the Brough up and down the coastline for half an hour or so. Nothing to see or do, and as the clouds were banking up in a very threatening fashion, we decided to nip back to London while the going was good. I took over the steering for the first half of the trip and Mike occupied the chair.

I had got the hang of the outfit properly now and was sailing past cars and other riders with gay abandon. Half-way home we changed round once more and it was my turn to occupy the chair. Just in time, too. As we turned into the main London road a flurry of snow swept through the wrecked windscreen. I hastily squeezed to one side of the sidecar and took refuge behind the remaining celluloid. That was better. The snow kept falling all the way to London.

Instead of frost on the roads we now had a layer of slimy dampness to contend with, but the Brough sailed over it with the same contempt as she had shown for frost and snow. When we reached Dorset House I struggled out of the sidecar and said "Good-night" to Harton. The tail lamp of the Brufsup vanished round the corner, and for some seconds I could just hear the note of her rumbling exhaust floating back. I do not suppose I shall ever see her again and certainly never drive her again, but what a machine ! It is a thousand pities that the number of makers of big vee-twins has dwindled. But—who knows?—perhaps George Brough has some wonderful S.S.120 hidden away at Nottingham. If he has, and it ever comes on the market, I shall have my name well up on the order list !

Passenger's view from the sidecar. Note the Awful Effect of travelling at speed with a cracked windscreen

An early Brooklands paddock shot of the Brough outfit in unblown form. Barry is in the saddle and Arthur Harber in the sidecar

Barry's Big Blown Brough

Story of a Famous Vee-twin Now Out to Grass with a Vintage Enthusiast

By VIC WILLOUGHBY

TO the scientific mind, the night of December 31-January 1 is no different from any other night. However, since that night marks the transition from one calendar year to the next, it is customary for folk to indulge in uncommon activities classified as "seeing the old year out" and "seeing the new year in." My way of conforming with the tradition on the last day of 1953 ranks, I consider, for the "uncommon" category—the departing year was ushered out at Silverstone, to the thunderous roar of a supercharged 996 c.c. Brough Superior-J.A.P., both with and without sidecar.

There is something special—even revered—about this particular outfit. More than a quarter of a century old, it is now the proudest possession of C. E. ("Tich") Allen, founder-member of the Vintage M.C.C. In its prime the Brough and sidecar enjoyed a long and illustrious racing career, mostly at Brooklands—first in the strong hands of its creator E. C. E. Baragwanath and, after his retirement from racing, with Noel Pope aboard.

From its very first season's racing, the highest honours fell to Barry's Brough outfit ("Barry" is the affectionate nickname by which Baragwanath is widely known). World's records, victories in sprint trials and short- and long-distance track races, a Brooklands Gold Star (for lapping at over 100 m.p.h.) and the Brook-

lands sidecar lap record—all these were numbered among the Brough's successes while Barry was in its saddle.

With Pope at the helm, the Brough collected further distinctions in sprint trials and on the Brooklands concrete bowl. There it earned for its new owner a sidecar Gold Star and, in solo trim, one of the only two motor cycle Double Gold Stars for lapping the track in excess of 120 m.p.h. (The other D.G.S. was achieved by the late Eric Fernihough.) When the Hitler war sounded the death-knell of Brooklands in 1939, the evergreen Brough was still king of the outer circuit, for Pope held both solo and sidecar lap records; the former was a tremendous achievement with a speed of more than 124 m.p.h. About 10 years later, bereft of its sidecar and enclosed in a streamlined shell, the Brough was still making headline news. Pope took it to the Utah salt flats in America, in quest of the world's fastest motor cycle speed record; he spilled, without serious hurt, at more than 100 m.p.h. . . .

Now, "Tich" Allen has restored the Brough outfit to virtually the same specification and condition in which it was most widely known during Barry's period of ownership, namely, in supercharged form. The Vintage Club dedicates itself to preserving pre-1931 machines in running condition, "in order that a new generation can marvel at the handiwork of the pioneers and an older generation can once again view with nostalgia the machines they rode in days gone by."

Exploits at Brooklands

The history of Barry's Big Blown Brough, as it is popularly called, is a saga of enterprise, endeavour and achievement. Though Barry has now seen 70 summers, his exploits with his outfit at Brooklands are remembered by many contemporary enthusiasts who are still on the right side of 40; this for the very good reason that Barry scorned to put away his leathers until he was 50 years old. He started racing, at Brooklands in 1912, on a 976 c.c. Winnit-J.A.P. fitted with one of the famous old "90-bore" engines. The story of the Brough, however, takes us back no farther than 1927. That period, recalls Barry with a nostalgic twinkle in his eye, was the heyday of the bonus system.

Attractive rewards were paid by numerous oil and accessory companies to race winners and record breakers. Among most competitors at that time there was an unwritten agreement to win races and break records by small margins. A big-gap win did not escape the race mathematicians, who saw to it that the handicap was suitably modified for subsequent races. And record-breaking by the lowest acceptable margin meant that, for a given increase in speed, there would be many bites at the financial cherry. In Brooklands handicap races, it was the job of Barry's sidecar passenger to count competitors as they were passed, so that the unforgivable crime of using too much speed was avoided.

During the lucrative years, successful racers spent their vacations in Austria, the South of France and other expensive resorts. But, largely because of abuse, the bonus system was eventually curtailed, and the Brooklands brigade faced hard times.

At that time, Barry had his own motor engineering business in the Camden Town district of London. He was already a devotee of the one-litre, big-twin engine and envisaged a racing sidecar outfit propelled by one of these mighty power units. He also had a firm faith in the safe steering qualities which George Brough was then building into his frames. Consequently, a 996 c.c. 8/50 racing J.A.P. engine was installed in a Brough frame with a Castle, bottom-link front fork. A Sturmey-Archer 3-speed model LS gear box and 4-plate clutch were entrusted with the task of transmitting the engine power to the rear wheel. Gear change was by hand.

Sidecar Experiments

After experiments at Brooklands with three Heywood chassis, Barry eventually selected one with a 30in track, since this was found to give the most satisfactory handling when wrenching the outfit round the full-bore, bumpy, right-hand bend at the Vickers sheds. A four-point chassis attachment was used. Hudsons Motors supplied the pointed-nose Tornado body which Barry used throughout 1927 and 1928, except for the Brooklands 200-mile races of those years; for these events he borrowed from J.A.P.s a bulbous-nose body which had previously been used by H. Le Vack.

For 1929 Barry decided to construct his own sidecar body, with minimum windage as the primary consideration. He hit on the bright idea of copying the shape of one of the floats of a seaplane exhibited in the South Kensington Science Museum. The age-old expedient of tipping the attendant ensured that inquisitive schoolboys were kept away, and also resulted in a step ladder being provided to enable Barry to take measurements.

The body was eventually beaten from aluminium sheet; it had an ash floor, and weighed 19lb 6oz. Its dimensions were slim for it was required to accommodate only the prone form of Barry's slightly-built passenger, Arthur Harber. A Brooklands regulation stipulated that sidecar passengers must have their heads and shoulders outside the sidecar body; a small cutaway in the top rear surface of the aluminium shell enabled the passenger to comply with this requirement while lying prone, though Brooklands stewards were at first sceptical.

All three wheels were of 21in diameter. The rear and sidecar wheels were of disc type thought to reduce wind drag; a conventional spoked wheel was retained at the front since it was found that, in a gusty wind, a disc made high-speed steering tricky. Track tyres were used at Brooklands, the rear one being of 3.5in section while those on the front and sidecar wheels were of 3in section. For sprint trials, where the paramount need was greater traction, a studded-tread rear tyre was fitted. In the search for still more grip, each stud was undercut below its leading edge with a razor blade so that the tyre presented a series of knife-edges of rubber to the road surface; additionally the tyre was run at a lowish pressure. The fact that these expedients militated against long tyre life was of little consequence since the tyres were supplied free; what was important was that standing-start getaways were improved.

As to the engine, Barry had his own ideas on induction layout. Two right-angle gas elbows, costing 8d each, were screwed to the inlet ports with their open ends facing to the left; to these were attached two Amac TT25 carburettors. Air intakes were staggered and opened into a common cylindrical box lying alongside the cylinder heads. The rear end of the box was open to atmosphere while two-thirds of the front end was blanked off, the remaining one-third being gauze-covered.

Alcohol-base fuels were always used, R.D.1 being the blend chosen for short-distance track races, and R.D.2 for long-distance events. With these fuels a compression ratio of 12.5 to 1 was employed. For sprints, the engine was built to a compression ratio of 14 to 1 and run on special "brew." Main jet sizes were around No. 70 (old rating) though that in the front carburettor was the larger by about two sizes to combat an inexplicable tendency to overheating of the front cylinder. Fuel consumption was no more than 10 m.p.g.

This view shows the supercharger, its drive and the induction system as rebuilt by C. E. ("Tich") Allen

That was the outfit which Barry raced and developed for the four seasons, 1927-1930 inclusive. On it he became as well-known for his spectacular negotiation of the Brooklands outer circuit as he was for the incongruity of the wing collar which he always wore beneath his leathers. Spectators loved to watch him fight the outfit's upward slides all round the rim of the Members' and Byfleet bankings, to see the Brough leap in the air over the vicious bumps on the drop to the Railway Straight, and to marvel at the strength of wrists and steel as Barry hugged the edge of the track in a protracted, full-bore slide past the Vickers sheds.

During this period engine tuning progressed along contemporary lines. The cam contours were modified on a bench grinder to increase the overlap from the standard 35 degrees to 60 degrees. The flywheels were lightened to aid snap acceleration. No revmeter was fitted; Barry's practice was to snatch through to the next gear, with the throttle wide open, as soon as the valves started to float, which he estimated was at about 6,500 r.p.m.

At Brooklands, in October 1927, he broke the world's sidecar

Allen, in the sidecar, declines to adopt the prone position and looks anything but comfortable as Vic Willoughby gives the Brough its head at Silverstone

A wonderful impression of Noel Pope's historic Brooklands lap at over 124 m.p.h.

decided to try his hand at supercharging. The frame was returned to George Brough for the engine mountings to be moved rearward by 1½in and the front down tube bent to make room for the blower in front of the engine.

Barry obtained a new 8/50 engine from J.A.P.s and put it into the altered frame. A No. 8 Powerplus supercharger was fitted between extended, light-alloy front engine plates; the mounting was eccentric to provide for adjustment of the driving chain. The supercharger was fed by a specially made, car-type Amal carburettor which was mounted beneath it and protected by a thin metal shield. Fuel was supplied to the three-jet carburettor by two pipes of no less than 5/16in bore; the reason for these generous dimensions is provided by the fuel consumption of the blown oufit—a mere 4 m.p.g.

No pressure release valve was incorporated in the induction system—Barry did not believe in using power to drive a supercharger and then blowing some of the results to the four winds. Blower speed was about 8 per cent below engine speed for track races; for sprint trials it was stepped up to engine speed. For these short-distance bursts it was also Barry's custom to weaken the carburation slightly, since the accent then was on sheer power and clean acceleration rather than long-distance reliability.

Ground from a solid steel billet, the cams gave less overlap than those for the unblown engine. Early tests at Brooklands revealed a pronounced tendency for the front cylinder to overheat—so much so that it was impossible to complete a single lap on full throttle. Barry attributed this trouble to the fact that the supercharger was building up pressure in the induction system for 410 degrees of crankshaft rotation before the front inlet valve opened, as against only 310 degrees in the case of the rear cylinder (the included angle of the cylinders was 50 degrees). To cure the trouble, he ground 1/16in off the peak of the front inlet cam and reduced the compression ration of the front cylinder from 7 to 1 to 6.8 to 1. At a later date a new cylinder head having a smaller-diameter inlet valve was fitted to restrict still further the filling of the front cylinder. I cannot escape the thought that there might have been something to say in favour of a pressure release valve, after all!

Pushrod Trouble

Another early bother was buckling of the exhaust pushrods. The solution was to use pushrods made from 7/16in-diameter steel tubing sleeved with ⅛in-diameter light-alloy tubing. With the exception that Martlet pistons, having 13/16in-diameter gudgeon pins, were fitted, the remainder of the engine was standard.

As with the unblown engine, no rev-meter was used, but Barry says that peak power was produced at about 5,200 r.p.m. To transmit the increased power and torque of the blown engine, a special heavyweight Sturmey Archer 3-speed gear box with 5-plate clutch was employed. Barry says the blower completely transformed the characteristics of the engine, quite apart from increasing its potency. Power delivery was rendered much sweeter and more tractable, and vibration was eliminated.

In this new and imposing form, the Brough outfit served Barry for the last three seasons of his racing career. During that period he estimates that it covered some 200 laps of the Brooklands outer circuit at speeds in excess of 100 m.p.h., taking into account practice laps as well as races. On his first appearance there in 1931, he was successful in gaining his long-sought Gold Star. Since the outfit's maximum speed then exceeded 110 m.p.h., however, it was

records for kilometre and mile, standing start, with average speeds of 74.96 and 80.5 m.p.h. respectively. Two years later he improved these figures to 75.74 and 83.32 m.p.h. in spite of the fog which lay over the track that day. His maximum speed, which he always geared to achieve at half-distance in standing-start bursts, was then around 106 m.p.h. In each of the four seasons under review he won the Brooklands Aggregate Cup for the sidecar class and, except for 1927 when he finished second to Freddy Dixon, he won the 5-lap Sidecar Championship race each year. More than 18 minutes was the margin by which he won the 200-mile sidecar race in 1928 at a speed of nearly 74 m.p.h. In 1930 he came within an ace of winning his Gold Star, when he lapped at 99 m.p.h.

The Brough was an equally formidable performer at the sprint meetings which were popular in those days; it was successful at Southport, Brighton, Lewes, Essingdon, and Lowestoft. At the last-named venue in 1927, Barry returned a one-way, standing-start, kilometre speed in excess of the existing world's sidecar record. It was this achievement which inspired his successful world's record attempt at Brooklands in October that year.

Towards the close of the 1930 season, the four-year-old J.A.P. engine blew up. So thorough was the disintegration that a rebuild was just not worth while. A new unit was called for and Barry

A vintage outfit with a proud history—the blown Brough as it is today

Using a bulbous-nose sidecar, Barry competes in a 200-mile Brooklands race more than 25 years ago

The extremely slim aspect of both machine and sidecar is apparent from this photograph

not surprising that its handling over the severe bumps on the drop to the Railway Straight had become rather uncertain. Steepening the steering-head angle by five degrees restored the steering to its previous excellence.

Sprint trials were then becoming fewer in number; consequently, Brooklands was the scene of the majority of the Brough's activities. Its lap speeds advanced by about 1 m.p.h. per year and, in 1933, Barry raised the sidecar record to 103.97 m.p.h. during an attempt to average 100 m.p.h. for a 3-lap, standing-start race. This objective was narrowly missed with a race speed of 99.22 m.p.h. In the 50-kilometre race during that season, Barry was, in fact, averaging more than the magic century from the standing start, but the gallop came to an unexpected end when an exhaust valve fractured on Lap 5.

The Brough outfit's fastest recorded half-mile speed in supercharged form was no less than 116.88 m.p.h.; this figure was achieved along the Railway Straight where the outfit was accelerating between the Members' and Byfleet bankings. During each of his last three seasons, Barry again won the 5-lap Sidecar Championship race and the Brooklands Aggregate Cup for his class. At the close of the 1933 season, he bowed graciously to that invincible opponent, Father Time, and sold the famous outfit to a rising Brooklands star—Noel Pope.

Meteoric Laps

Pope's first job, early in 1934, was to remove the sidecar, convert the gear change to foot operation, and take the supercharged solo to the Track for some trial lappery; straight away he circulated in excess of 100 m.p.h. Later that season he established a record at the Brighton Sprint Trials with a mean speed of over 80 m.p.h. for the standing-start half-mile, made best time of the day at the Gatwick sprints, and succeeded in pushing his Brooklands lap speeds up to 110 m.p.h.

During the following winter he worked hard on the engine. His own cams, giving more overlap, were made and installed. A boost gauge was fitted to the induction system as was a safety valve set to blow off at + 20lb sq in. Pope geared the blower to run faster than previously; it was driven at engine speed at Brooklands and at 1.3 times that speed for sprints. Boost pressures of + 10 to 12lb/sq in were commonly used. Various successes ensued in 1935 including a 100 m.p.h. Gold Star for the flying-kilometre on Southport sands. Most notable, however, was a meteoric Brooklands lap at more than 120 m.p.h. to break the solo lap record and win a coveted Double Gold Star. Pope patently had no interest in the little-by-little speed increases bred by the bonus system!

Another rebuild followed at the close of the season and, in 1936, the Brough emerged with bevel-driven twin B.T.-H. magnetos and two sparking plugs for each cylinder head. About this time, Pope was spending a good deal of time on the Continent road racing with the "Circus." Hence in 1936 and 1937 his outings with the Brough became less frequent. Nevertheless, on its occasional appearances, the blown monster recorded more best times at Saltburn and Gatwick, and collected places at Brooklands.

Sidecar Successes

In preparation for 1938, the annual winter overhaul included the fitting of even more severe cams and a new Castle bottom-link front fork. The long-discarded sidecar was refitted, and Pope won his first race at near-lap-record speed. In the process he won his sidecar Gold Star and, from a flying start, covered 10 kilometres, unofficially timed, in excess of the then current world's record. The following week, he shattered the sidecar lap record with a speed of 106.6 m.p.h. Once again the Brough, without sidecar, recorded best time of the meeting at Gatwick.

Pope planned to attack the world's motor cycle speed record in 1939; for this purpose he again employed the Brough. The old 8/50 J.A.P. engine was retired; in its place went one of the latest 8/80 units having both exhaust ports facing forward. The outbreak of war foiled Pope's world's-record plans, but not before he had proved his mettle with that fantastic and heroic Brooklands lap at 124.5 m.p.h. Another record smashed was that for the Gatwick quarter-mile sprint. Pope's time of 11.53 seconds represented a mean speed of more than 78 m.p.h.—this from a virtual standing start.

Fore nine years the Brough lay idle. When it was next pressed into service, at Redcar, it recorded the customary best time, but Pope had his mind set on bigger things. He still cherished world's-maximum ambitions and, in 1949, he enclosed the Brough in a beautiful-looking streamlined shell and set sail for America. On the wide open spaces of the Utah Salt Lake he came face to face with the aerodynamic perils confronting the fully streamlined two-

wheeler. A crash at three-figure speed ended his valiant effort.

That episode concluded the Brough's serious racing career which had started more than 20 years earlier. The legendary model was put aside until, just over a year ago, "Tich" Allen persuaded Pope to part with it. The third chapter of its history opened.

Allen's interest in the Brough is purely historical; it takes pride of place among some half-dozen old machines in his collection. He believes it is the only blown vintage model in existence.

Bound by the chronological limits of the Vintage Club's charter, Allen has restored the Brough outfit as nearly as possible to its specification at the end of 1930. To do this he has consulted Barry on innumerable points, and has made a detailed study of all the relevant photographs he has been able to acquire. He bought the outfit without an engine but built up an 8/50 from Barry's old spares and parts cannibalized from Allen's own Brough Superior "Pendine" model. A No. 8 Powerplus supercharger took six months to locate, for these blowers have been out of production for 20 years!

The work was completed last October, and the old outfit made its appearance that month at the Vintage Club's Thruxton sprint meeting. Clutch-drag made it impossible to disengage bottom gear once the outfit was on the move; in that gear alone the standing-start quarter-mile was covered in 17.8 seconds. Eagerly, though not without due reverence, I accepted an invitation to ride the Brough outfit after Christmas.

Fun at Silverstone

When first I saw it, I pounced on the Brough with a steel measuring tape; the wheelbase was 60½in, the track 35in and the sidecar-wheel spindle was 8in forward of the rear-wheel spindle. The ultra-slim sidecar body was supported on two quarter-elliptic springs at the rear, and twin coil springs at the front. Allen told me the gear ratios were 3.25, 4.5 and 6 to 1.

While the Brough's preparation was a masterpiece of historical accuracy, I felt that its mechanical state was such that "Tich" Allen would doubtless be able to improve it given a little more time and experience. Engine starting on alcohol proved difficult, and required the used of a tow-rope; filling the carburettor with benzole and priming the induction pipe with the same fuel gave much more satisfactory results. Carburation at small throttle openings and low r.p.m. was uncertain, and the highest boost-gauge reading obtained was + 2lb/sq in.

Nevertheless, once the engine was cracking on full throttle and sufficient r.p.m., I was able to gain a clear impression of the model's characteristics. The power was smooth, lusty and effortless; it built up remarkably as the r.p.m. increased and the blower thus became more effective. After I had done a few laps of the Silverstone Club circuit with Allen taking his punishment in the sidecar, he complained that the exhaust note wrought havoc with his eardrums. During the afternoon, he demonstrated the quick detachability of the sidecar and we rode the Brough in solo form. Either as a sidecar outfit or as a solo, the Brough is not intended to negotiate small-radius corners rapidly; it is an uncompromising, straight-ahead projectile with a very strong self-centring action to its steering.

To my regret, we had no accurate means of assessing the Brough's speed though Allen, for the fun of the thing, had mounted an air-speed indicator on the handlebar! Flat in second gear (for, in top, the model was overgeared for Silverstone) I got steady readings of 100 and 120 m.p.h. respectively with and without the sidecar. Rapid fluctuations of the indicator needle some 20 m.p.h. farther up the scale underlined the instrument's unsuitability for measuring terrestrial speeds!

Such is the story of Barry's Big Blown Brough. Its deeds have earned it an immortal place in the pages of British motor cycle racing history.

In The Grand Manner

John Griffith Writes of a Trip by Brough Superior Across Six Miles of London—via Nottingham!

Bright interval at Oakham, countytown of Rutland, England's smallest county. Passenger Ike Webb (left) is dry; Allen and Griffith are as yet only slightly damp.

FLANNEL, according to the Concise Oxford Dictionary, is "open woollen stuff, usually without nap." According to the Editor, it is also the method employed by his staff to borrow highly desirable machinery from friends in and out of the trade. Notwithstanding this, he was kind enough to agree that it would be a good idea to go to Nottingham and collect E. O. "Blackie" Blacknell's Brough Superior and sidecar in order to visit Pride and Clarke's South London showrooms (some half-dozen miles from the office) wherein a special display of Blacknell wares is now on view.

Now this is no ordinary outfit (come to that, no B.-S. could ever be dubbed "ordinary"). The sidecar is the very first-off Blacknell, built just after the war for "Blackie's" own smoking. So great was the clamour for replicas that, some-

what reluctantly, "Blackie" decided to go into the sidecar trade—and that's the story behind the name Blacknell!

Originally the chair was hitched to the very last Brough SS100 to leave the Nottingham works, just after the end of the war. In a moment of aberration "Blackie" sold this machine, JTO828, and has regretted it ever since. However, southern sales representative for Blacknell Sidecars, Ltd., is C. E. "Tich" Allen, founder of the Vintage Club and another worshipper at the B.-S. shrine, and last year he found an immaculate 1938 SS100, as near as makes no odds, identical with the post-war model. The old "Bullett" sidecar was hauled out of the loft where it had been stored for some years and refurbished to its original specification, and the marriage was completed.

"Tich" actually suggested that I should drive the outfit down to Pride and Clarke. He agreed to come along, too, with his 1933 1,150 c.c. side-valve B.-S. to which was hitched the prototype model of the very latest "San Remo" Blacknell two-seater saloon. To complete the party, Ike Webb, director and manager of Blacknell Sidecars, Ltd., would ride in the "San Remo" and see if it was as comfortable as he believed.

This picture illustrated the late Charlie Markham's story in 1947 and shows him at speed with the sidecar attached to the original SS100. Below, right, is the power unit of the current SS100.

My journey to Nottingham took place in excellent weather and a train. The return, with the outfits, took place in the open and in the rain. The clerk of the weather definitely has me on the list. I collected an outfit from Blackpool a few years ago and read later that the day on which I drove it to London had been the coldest for a century. Now I find that the trip with the " Bruff-Sups " was made on the wettest April day for 72 years!

The day dawned bright and cheerful, but by the time the party had assembled at one of Blacknell Motors' showrooms it was raining lightly. Photographer Harry Roberts did not mind the weather; he was in his " utility." Ike did not mind the weather; he was in the saloon sidecar. " Blackie " did not mind the weather; he wasn't coming. What " Tich " and I thought about the weather doesn't really matter.

" Tich's " 11-50 has a beefy J.A.P. motor, possibly the biggest ever fitted to

Temporary change of mounts—Allen on the SS100 and Griffith on the 11-50 woofle away from their lunch stop at Bedford.

Journey's end: Ike Webb is welcomed by George Lyle, manager of the Pride and Clarke sidecar department.

a British production machine. Solo top gear is 3.5 : 1—and it was on solo gearing! Despite this, " Tich " was soon cracking along at some 50-55 m.p.h. with occasional bursts at 60. I must admit that I had expected a 45 m.p.h. cruising speed, for the 26-year-old machine was hauling, remember, a large two-seat chair with one heavy passenger.

To the passenger-less SS100, this gait was kid's stuff. A gentle booming from the twin fishtails was all I could hear. Hills called for a fractional movement of the right wrist, very slow corners could be taken easily in top provided the ignition, controlled by left-hand twist-grip, was retarded a mite. Flexibility was fantastic. The 1,000 c.c. o.h.v. Matchless engine could be throttled back to 15 m.p.h., retarded, in top, and then accelerated away again with no fuss or snatch, yet if both grips were twirled rapidly the chariot would leap down the road in fine style. The outfit is " Blackie's " pride and joy, so I did not attempt to find the mean maximum speed

in top—at 75 m.p.h. there was more coming, but I shut off; I don't expect the motor would have burst, but my face would have been red if it had!

Comfort was every bit as good as with the best of modern machines. This, I suspect, was the result not only of the plunger rear springing, but of an excellent, low riding position and well-sprung pan-type saddle. But I could have done without the Pagusa pillion, which is mounted so that its handle scratches the driver's back for him! The outfit steered hands-off and handling on corners left nothing to be desired. Maybe it's the long, low machine, maybe it's the Castle forks—whatever the cause, a Brough with chair has no peer for handling.

Just outside Melton Mowbray, the rain eased up a little so, as it was spring, we stopped to let Harry snap us in front of a tree in blossom. A pathetic gesture. It was an English spring and we were doomed to be showered on all the way home. The rain set in again and we did not halt in the pretty little village of

Uppingham, but pressed on to our lunch stop at Bedford.

After lunch we said our good-byes to Harry—off home to Coventry—and I took over the 11-50. Handling was as good as on the SS100—but a loose saddle-nose pivot took the edge off the enjoyment. I found that the outfit was quite happy with its high gear—no protests from the engine and no big throttle openings for speeds up to 60 m.p.h. On hills, third was frequently used—in fact, " Tich " says he has top as an overdrive.

So through London and its traffic—a good tick-over is a godsend there and the SS100 has one—to the sidecar department of Pride and Clarke's, where manager George Lyle was waiting to welcome us. We had been out in the rain for several hours. Apart from soaked gloves and goggles, I was dry. A " Tuffler " scarf had prevented water penetrating onto an ordinary scarf worn under it, and " Gisenia " overtrousers and Armadrake " Viscount " coat had kept me perfectly comfortable.

The original Brough Superior/Blacknell outfit was described by my predecessor, the late Charlie Markham, in an article entitled " You'd Like George! ", in September, 1947. I can do no better than repeat his words: " The cult of the ' Bruff-Sup ' is not merely a hankering after class distinction—it is true appreciation of something striving to be ' a little better than the best '."

If you would like to see " George's " half-brother, he is on show, with a special display of Blacknell sidecars, from today for a fortnight at the sidecar department of Pride and Clarke, Ltd., Stockwell Road, Brixton, London, S.W.9. Pride and Clarke's have several hundred motorcycles and sidecars for sale—and one not for sale. This is it!

Built for Speed No. 19

JOHN GRIFFITH describes

IN BRIEF

Engine: 50° V-twin s.v. J.A.P.; 85 mm. bore × 85 mm. stroke=976 c.c.; no b.h.p. or c.r. figures available.

Fuel Tank: Steel, 1½ gal. capacity.

Oil: Carried in nose section of fuel tank, 2 pt.

Wheels: Steel rims carrying 3.00-in. × 28-in. beaded-edge tyres, Goodyear front, Dunlop rear.

Weight: Approx. 250 lb.

'OLD BILL'

GEORGE BROUGH'S PERSONAL BROUGH

SUPERIOR SPRINTER OF THE EARLY TWENTIES

Those present : (l. to r.) George Morris, "Titch" Allen, "Blackie" Blacknell, George Brough, John Griffith, Frank Inger and Ike Webb.

"FIFTY-ONE firsts in a row and then the backside torn out of my trousers." That is George Brough's own terse account of the astounding run of success achieved by him and his 1922-23 Brough Superior sprint and hill-climb machine "Old Bill"—so called after Bruce Bairnsfather's cartoon character of World War One.

The surface which put an abrasive end to this brilliant partnership was that of the course at Clipstone, near Mansfield, on the momentous occasion in 1923 when the front tyre burst as "Old Bill" was on full song. By the time George had mended sufficiently to ride notwithstanding, he had built a better machine, forerunner of the SS 100 with o.h.v. motor, and s.v.-engined "Old Bill" was pensioned off.

C. E. "Titch" Allen, founder of the Vintage M.C.C., has the very pleasant hobby of rooting out old B.-S. machines which won especial fame in their day, and rebuilding them. The latest is "Old Bill."

"Titch" does not believe in rebuilding and letting lie—he contrives to get a lot of enjoyment from his period pieces. So it was that, a few weeks ago, we all met on that historic course at Clipstone—"Old Bill," George, "Titch," Ike Webb (who used to be George's chief frame builder and now looks after the Blacknell sidecar-building shop), E. O. "Blackie" Blacknell, and Frank Inger and George Morris, of

Mansfield, who were present when "Old Bill" crashed.

In those days the course had a reasonable surface; now it is somewhat pot-holed and a housing estate has sprung up around it. It is still a private drive and the owner, who came down to see our party, was kind enough to give us the O.K. to try "Old Bill" on the scene of his youthful rampage.

Thirty-six years is a long time. "The start was here." "No, it was here by these gates." Opinions differed strongly. I was tickled pink when a local chap told the now loudly arguing contingent that the gates had been moved . . . !

Starting "Old Bill" calls for the traditional technique. With the proud owner aboard, he was pushed off. The engine fired and the pushers proceeded to pick themselves up. "Titch" disappeared up the drive with some alacrity. What a crackle! The bellow from the open pipes was in complete contrast to what one would expect of a side-valve engine: there was more to this motor than met the eye.

"Titch" returned and George had a go. Now, shall we say, *approaching* middle-age. George still has a twinkle in his eye and lead in his right glove. He shot off like a scalded cat, the rear wheel spinning and squirming under full throttle. After several runs he was fast finding his old sprinting form (although he had many quite unrepeatable things to say about the saddle, a temporary affair with an embarrassing habit of tilting backwards when one struck a bump).

Then my turn came. What a bike this was —no megaphoning present-day racer but a machine with punch, like the later speedway J.A.P. jobs, right from the bottom end of the range, and right up to the top end too. Handling was amazingly good. Even when I hit a pot-hole on full throttle when accelerating in top, the only indications of it were a momentary clash of the forks and a more permanent dent in the rear rim.

Regretfully, "time" had to be called and we returned to our headquarters for lunch and reminiscences, by Ike and George, of the Golden Age of Motorcycling.

And now for a portrait of "Old Bill."

The engine, a J.A.P. twin of 1,000 c.c.,

George guns "Old Bill" away from the start on the piece of road which he so vividly remembers from the early 'twenties. This time he stayed on!

is a prototype of the "four-cam" 8/30, so called because it was nominally of 8 h.p. and actually produced 30 b.h.p.

The top of the crankcase has been machined away so that the cylinder bases are below the level of the timing chest, giving a higher-than-standard c.r.; compression is also augmented by deep valve-port caps which, when screwed home, almost touch the valves when the latter are fully open. Everything in the motor is highly polished and the con-rods are much lightened but not drilled.

Tulip-type valves are used in conjunction with solid cam-followers; the 8/30 had roller followers. Mains and big-end bearings are all of roller pattern. Each flywheel is machined from a single steel billet and comprises a rim with an integral diametrical

spoke which carries the mainshaft and big-end; normal disc-type flywheels were used on standard engines.

A Lucas 50° magneto and Binks "Mouse-trap" carburetter are fitted. Other features are a three-speed close-ratio Sturmey Archer gearbox, heavyweight racing Webb forks and heavy struts to stiffen the frame.

The original rear wheel had a 26-in. rim and dummy belt-rim brake, but a 28-in. wheel with hub brake is now fitted. Both the front and the rear wheel, however, still have beaded-edge rims.

What are "Titch's" intentions with regard to "Old Bill"? Strictly honourable. He hopes to air him at a sprint or two for the enjoyment and education of all concerned. What price a quarter in less than 16 seconds?

*Close-ups of the works: note the Binks "Mouse-trap" carburetter, **the** frame strengthening struts and the liberal drilling.*

Old Bill—Ike's

By Vic Willoughby

GEORGE BROUGH'S ONCE INVINCIBLE SIDE-VALVE RACER PUTS THE CLOCK BACK NEARLY 40 YEARS

Ike Webb

TO anyone but Ike Webb, a span of 40 years is pretty well a lifetime. But bring Ike face to face with Old Bill—the 980 c.c. side-valve vee-twin racing Brough Superior he nursed around 1922-3—and the intervening years vanish faster than a dream. Straight off the cuff he quotes sprocket and jet sizes; and he breaks out in a sweat at the sight of all those lightening holes, as if it were only yesterday he was bruising his ribs on the breast drill.

King-pin of sprint and hill climb in the last years before engines with valves in the attic finally ousted the simple side-valve from the stronghold of speed, Old Bill was the exclusive projectile of the illustrious George Brough, maker of massive whispering twins, acknowledged the world over as the Rolls Royce of motor cycles. And a more satisfying medium for self expression George could scarcely have conceived.

For Old Bill was not only the first side-valve to clock 100 m.p.h. at Brooklands. Oh, no. In 51 consecutive meetings, solo and sidecar, he dwarfed the opposition by making fastest time of the day. And the 52nd f.t.d. was in the bag when the front tyre burst.

That was on the perilously narrow, gravel-surfaced Clipston sprint strip. With the finish line looming up at nearly a ton, George and Old Bill parted spectacularly. As Ike recalls it, the bike or the rider (or both) crossed the line in f.t.d. But Freddy Dixon, next-fastest on his Harley, protested they should have done so together, not independently! And so the Brough's last race was a moral if not an official victory.

Save perhaps for George, no one knows Broughs in general or Old Bill in particular better than Ike Webb—71 years young and as lively as a cricket. He built the first and last Broughs, clocked 175,000 miles on one of his own, but loved none better than Old Bill. And if George's record isn't testimony enough of the getaway, there is Titch Allen's 18.6s for the standing-start quarter-mile at Wellesbourne—running on super-premium petrol instead of the more exotic RD1 alcohol of the vintage years and hauling a sidecar ballasted by 14 stones of Phil Heath!

Vintage-fan Allen it was who rescued Old Bill from decay and refurbished him; and who, to my delight, invited me to Mallory Park to try the old warrior. And ancient though he may be, Old Bill still chuckles throatily and leaves unsuspecting pushers-off flat on their faces as the clutch goes home.

The hump of his torque curve is way over to the left; and with no more weight than the bare and very spindly essentials he scorns a delicate touch on the clutch lever. You just drop it like a hot potato and the 50-degree J.A.P. engine does the rest—except, that is, for changing up whenever the valves float (by hand in George's time) and wrestling with the 3ft-wide handlebar as George had to at top speed on the shattering bumps of his day.

That was the heyday of the rider-tuner and Brough was one of the shrewdest. In these scientific times, when the tyre boffins have to concoct a special tread mix to harness the colossal punch of George Brown's Nero and George has to lengthen the wheelbase to keep the plot from becoming a moon-probe, a three-speed side-valve seems a crude sort of racer. But what the old-timers lacked in academic knowledge they made up in enthusiasm, ingenuity and craftsmanship.

Top: Vic Willoughby has Old Bill flat in second. Here Titch Allen samples a modern solo for a change—George Salt's Ariel Sports Arrow

Typical was the quest for a high compression ratio in an engine which seems specifically designed to make it impossible. The crankcase mouths were machined and filed down until the part-conical piston crowns all but fouled the non-detachable cylinder heads; and the shoulders of the valve caps were cut back till the valves had only bare room for full lift. Eventually the ratio reached nearly 8 to 1 and the combustion-chamber shape must have been a boffin's nightmare. But alcohol fuel prevented detonation—at a cost. Old Bill ran only nine miles on a gallon, and, says Ike, called for a refill after a pre-race warm-up.

Initially, the engine was one of Bert Le Vack's two prototypes for the four-cam 8/30 J.A.P. With bore and stroke measuring 85.7 x 85mm, it is near enough square; and when it was passed to George Brough the other prototype, a long-stroke, went to pre-war sidecar star Ted Baragwanath.

One of the first things George did was

Above: Loose surfaces were common in Old Bill's day; so, with Allen helpless in the aluminium capsule, Willoughby scatters the gravel in Mallory Park's paddock. Below is the Binks mousetrap carburettor

to fit a pair of polished steel flywheels so light they consisted merely of the rim and a spoke to take the crankpin and mainshafts! Other starkly functional features were a Binks mousetrap carburettor (then the recognized wear for short races) and valve timing giving an unheard-of 65 degrees of overlap, but with the inlet-opening and exhaust-closing points fixed ten degrees later for the front cylinder than the rear.

Oiling? That consisted of an adjustable gravity drip-feed to the rear wall of the front cylinder and a spring-loaded plunger pump, charged by a handlebar lever and supplying another drip-feed to the rim of the crankcase. It was left to the flywheels to churn the oil around; those days, big ends had to fare as best they could!

Solo top gear was 4.1 to 1 and sidecar 4.6. And if you think those high, especially in view of the large-diameter rear tyre (28 x 3in), Ike doesn't. He calls to mind a 90-bore twin they raced solo in 1921 on the fantastic ratio of 2.78 to 1—and with a 28in tyre at that. At 65 per, says Ike, you could watch the valves dawdling up and down. Even so, a late refinement on Old Bill was a 26in wheel for courses calling for lower gearing.

I asked Ike about the ⅜in tubular struts from the front of the crankcase to the rear-wheel spindle and saddle nose. Those, it seems, were fitted to stop the diamond frame squirming under the engine's punch.

At Mallory I first tried Old Bill's high, slender, bullet-nose sidecar; not the actual capsule occupied in George Brough's day by the intrepid midget, George Vickers, but a similar device kindly loaned by Watsonians. In it I learned that, on full bore, the mousetrap carburettor blows as much fuel back in the passenger's face as it feeds to the engine. And when it was my turn to occupy the spartan saddle and span the enormous width of the handlebar, I dis-

covered that all George's and Ike's ingenuity had gone into making Old Bill go—not stop. That tobacco-tin front brake (and doubtless the original but now departed dummy belt-rim rear brake, too) was nothing more than a monstrous concession to auto-suggestion!

If Ike and Titch took me back nearly 40 years, it was George Salt who brought me up to date again. He turned up and offered me a flip on his Ariel Sports Arrow. You know the model—at least, you ought to. Ridden by Peter Inchley and Robin Good, it was second two-fifty in the Silverstone 1000, the Barcelona 24-hour Race and the Thruxton 500-miler.

What a contrast with Old Bill! From the seat the Arrow is almost inaudible, and at low revs it is as docile as a kitten. In Spain, though, both the note and power had much more kick; for the Barcelona regs are quite elastic and the standard silencers were ditched for racing-type expansion boxes.

But even muffled it's a honey. And with 2,500 near-trouble-free racing miles to its credit it runs as well as ever and dead smoothly. As the revs build up, so the power takes on a useful slant and you can let the engine buzz till the revs won't climb any higher. The only fly in the ointment is that the jump from bottom to second is so big that, however hard you buzz the engine first, it struggles a bit when you change up. But there again, the Spanish meeting allowed close-ratio gears, while the other two circuits don't call for bottom gear.

Of course, the Arrow just begs to be cranked over, and it's easy to understand why even a staid, retired racer such as ex-world champion Cecil Sandford just can't resist the annual call to a basinful of fun on a similar model at Thruxton. He's no mug!

208: TO GEORGE BROUGH

5.3.32   *Hythe, Southampton*

Dear Mr. Brough, It is the silkiest thing I have ever ridden: partly because of the perfect tune, partly from the high gear: but mostly because of the spring sprocket, I suppose. The gear is not too high. I can get down to 16 m.p.h.: and she pulls fairly at 30 m.p.h. and at 50 she is a dream. Just popples along so mildly that I can count the revs.

It was very cold but a beautiful ride. The back plug lasted till I got to Welwyn. The second plug is still running. I took two from your stores: so have made the cheque for 10/- extra, which I hope will cover them.

I think this is going to be a very excellent bike. The crowds that gape at her, just now, will stop looking after she gets dirty: and that may be soon, if only the R.A.F. give me spare time enough to use the poor thing.

I am very grateful to you and everybody for the care taken to make her perfect. Yours ever   T E SHAW.

Lawrence's eloquent praise of his Brough is reproduced from the book "Letters of T. E. Lawrence." Below: David Dixon tries the famous flier

VERY superior

by DAVID DIXON

JUST what T. E. Shaw—Lawrence of Arabia— thought of his new SS100 is shown in the letter (pictured above) to George Brough in 1932. Lawrence has long since become a legend. So have Brough Superiors. He owned a succession of these big twins for, like so many before him and after, it was on a motor cycle that he had found his outlet.

So far as is known, only one ex-Lawrence Brough is on the road today—the SS100 mentioned in the letter to George. And credit for preserving that historic machine must go to a 27-year-old Portsmouth enthusiast, Les Perrin.

Just how well he has succeeded I found out when I had my first Brough ride the other weekend. Brought up in the mystique of the Brough cult, perhaps I was expecting too much. A strange beast? Yes, very odd and not to be judged on first impressions, for this mount is older than I and comparisons with contemporary machines would be unfair.

But where was the magnetism of these old vee-twins, the attraction that lured discerning men like Lawrence into owning a succession of such models? In the thirties, roads were uncluttered and the tempo of life considerably slower than now. So judge the machine in that light and it glows.

I had parked a six-fifty Triumph Bonneville and straddled the Brough. What a comparison!

WAFFLING

The old 998 cc twin seemed to come right from the horseless carriage age; lots of mechanical clatter from the exposed valve gear, a totally strange waffling burble from the exhaust and an impression of being astride a garden gate hinged in the middle.

Unkind criticism? Yes, of course it is, but those were my initial reactions. To gain a more lasting impression, I went off for a gallop across Portsdown Hill, overlooking Portsmouth. The Brough gathered itself together through the gears —oh, that awkward hand-change—and on a mere whiff of gas it settled into a loping 50 mph stride.

Only a mellow burble from the twin exhausts and some valve clatter were audible as I was wafted along on the breeze of yesteryear. The sheer effortlessness and cotton-wool punch of the power unit were something I had never known before.

I longed to tweak the grip just a shade sharper, but the engine had hardly emerged from its overhaul . . . .

Then a corner loomed up— no, the Brough is definitely *not* the world's best roadholder! The pivoted-fork rear suspension—a revolutionary feature 30 years ago—ironed out the shocks on the straight, but a long wheelbase and lack of hydraulic damping at front and rear made each corner a fresh will-I-or-won't-I challenge. I judge Lawrence had real fun on the swervery.

Leisurely motoring 30 years ago was hardly a testing time for brakes, and the Brough's anchors, even with new linings, were way down on present-day standards.

JUST RIGHT

Particularly pleasing was the comfortable riding position. Perrin had discarded the Triumph dual-seat which the previous owner had fitted and substituted an original Lycett saddle and pillion. To many of us a saddle may sound archaic but, in fact, it was most comfortable. Especially the riding position — compact and with just enough forward lean.

The traditional silver-finish petrol tank was missing —damaged in an accident, as was the original headlamp, but

Above: Les Perrin checks the tappet clearances. Right: Adjusting the front-brake cable

Use of a short prop pivoted from under the footrest and well out from the centre of the machine ensures rigid support when the model is parked

Perrin hopes to find replacements soon. Also due for replacement later are the exhaust pipes; stainless-steel ones would match the twin silencers of the same material.

An Amal carburettor is the only other major item still short on the standard specification; it was replaced at some time by a Bowden. Otherwise, the spec is pretty well as original after two years of restoration by Perrin.

SURPRISE

Incidentally, as the original log book had been returned to a previous owner, Perrin did not know he had bought a Lawrence Brough—for £1! —as he towed the dilapidated heap away from a friend's garage. At that time a sidecar

The Brough is powered by a 998 cc JAP vee-twin engine. The present Bowden carburettor is to be replaced by an Amal

was fitted and only after discarding the old chair did he become curious and ask the registration authorities.

Yes, GW 2275 had belonged to T. E. Shaw, of 14, Barton Street, London, SW1. Perhaps you didn't know that when Lawrence had finished in the desert he joined the Air Force, then the Tank Corps where he adopted the name of Shaw, and finally returned to the Air Force as an aircraftsman.

Of course, the knowledge that he had a Lawrence Brough, probably the only one in existence, spurred on Perrin's res-

toration. Major mechanical component was a new big-end assembly, price £6 6s, for the JAP engine. Various other minor bits and pieces were required and some items, such as phosphor-bronze bushes and valve guides were made by friends.

Some ingenuity was required, too. Gudgeon pins were not obtainable; Les found a pair of Vauxhall car pins which were the right diameter but ¼in short. So he welded on extensions!

More ingenuity went into the fabrication of a main-shaft bearing for the Sturmey-Archer gear box. But the gears and clutch, even the chains, were in good order.

The Lawrence SS100 today. Chief departure from original is the petrol tank; the hunt for a traditional silver-finish one is still on

Stripping and cleaning before painting produced most of the sweat and toil. Two tins of Valspar enamel gave a high-gloss finish.

And what did all this cost? A mere £19! But you must remember that some of the parts, which would normally have to be bought retail, were made by friends in the trade, keeping the cost low.

And those of you with insurance problems might care to know that the Brough was covered for £5 10s. by the DA scheme. Incidentally, the model passed its MoT test first time.

As those who saw the Brough Superior Rally last month realize, there are plenty of old Broughs lovingly restored and well cared for roaming the roads.

But can any lick Perrin's for distinction?

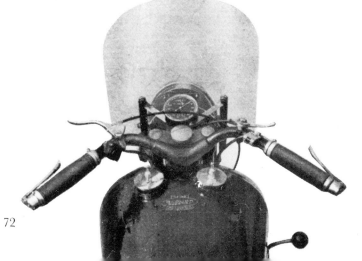

Brough Superior

. . . the expression of a cult of which
George Brough was the founder and high priest

THE ROLLS-ROYCE OF MOTOR CYCLES

vide The Motor Cycle

FIRST used in 1924, that slogan appeared in all Brough Superior literature until motorcycle production stopped in 1940. Proudly too because Rolls-Royce conceded that the Brough Superior was worthy of the slogan and withdrew their objection to its use . . . the only occasion on which the close guard on that famous trade name was relaxed.

Was this claim fact or fiction? Did the Brough Superior motorcycle bear comparison with the lordly Rolls-Royce? The argument split enthusiasts for 40 years.

Those who derided the claim . . . many jaundiced by sour grapes . . . said the Brough was an over-priced assembly of proprietary parts, J.A.P. engine, Sturmey Archer gearbox, etc., and that a similar assembly could be bought under a different name for two thirds the price.

The supporters . . . owners for the most part . . . maintained it was the best machine in the world and criticism tantamount to treason.

Now that more than 20 years have passed since the Brough was built it should be possible to discuss the matter objectively: I say should be because the Brough legend, far from passing into history, is evergreen, maintained by a new generation through the Brough Superior Owners Club. One unkind word of criticism and their wrath descends on the head of the unfortunate . . . as a writer on a weekly recently discovered.

How, then, did this assembly of parts . . . that description is agreed . . . become a legend in its lifetime and continue so when contemporaries and rivals vanished into limbo? The Brough's durability, actual and in reputation, is the proof of the pudding: so what was the recipe for a success story unique in the history of motorcycles?

The answer, I suggest, is one man's dedication to an ideal as distinct from the more common pursuit of commercial success. From the moment when the first B.S.—the true Brough Superior devotee always uses that abbreviation—was a mere gleam in G.B.'s (again note the abbreviation) mind's eye there was only one aim: to make his ideal machine. *His* machine, mark you. Seldom did the consideration of whether the public would buy intrude on B.S. policy, and history suggests that when there was a compromise it was a commercial failure. For the B.S. was never a commercial undertaking of the popular kind. Rather was it the expression of a cult of which G.B. was the founder and high priest. In the evolution of the machine one can follow the gradual maturing of the man . . . from the cheerful extrovert of the '20s to the seasoned connoisseur of the later '30s. So the story of the B.S. is the story of G.B., champion of the select Vintage band of designer-manufacturer riders.

In the case of G.B. you can add " P.R.O. and publicist "— though the purist may object to their use because the names, though not the function, were certainly not contemporary.

To get G.B. in perspective you have to go back a long way, to 1900 at least, when the schoolboy son of W. E. Brough, an engineer who had gone into the new fangled world of cars and motorcycles, learned to ride on the sink or swim system by " borrowing " one of his father's machines. By 1906 he had talked his way into riding one of his father's products, a 2½ h.p. single-gear model, in his first classic, the Land's End-John o' Groats. He pedalled most of the way!

In 1910, 11 and 12 he won the premier award in the London-Edinburgh-London M.C.C. trial, thereby winning the Challenge Cup outright. His time error for the final event was 10 seconds. In 1912 he rode a vee-twin single-gear Brough through the Scottish Six Days Trial, with sealed tool bags to make things more difficult, at a time when the competition man carried a mobile workshop astern. That was when he first decided that the vee-twin was the engine for him, and, incidentally, it marked the first difference of technical opinion with his father, who was sold on flat twins. Which leads me to the first of a " now it can be told " series for which I am deeply grateful to G.B. for " telling all " as they say in Sunday newspapers.

The records of the Isle of Man T.T. contain a laconic entry which has escaped most historians . . . Brough 1913 S.R.I. Interpreted, it means that in 1913 one Brough was entered in the Senior race and retired.

But what a story lies behind that brief entry. " It did not take me long," G.B. told me, " to realize that father's flat twin was no flier. But at that time Jack Emerson was breaking records at Brooklands with Granville Bradshaw's flat-twin A.B.C. which was the same size and shape. My mother talked father into letting me fit an A.B.C. engine for the T.T. and I went down to Weybridge to arrange the swap. When I went out on the track I was dismayed to find the A.B.C. was even worse. The slide rule experts stripped the engine but couldn't find anything wrong and it needed a lot of courage for a youngster like me to point out that because of a slip up in the casting the valve opening was masked. That fixed, the engine was quite good but I had no time to test it until I got to the Island.

"On the first practice run the flywheel spun off and the connecting rods tied themselves in a knot. You can imagine how I felt but Freddie Barnes, the Zenith Gradua maker, offered me one of his spare machines. The stewards finally agreed to the change providing we painted 'Zenith-Brough' on the tank. In the race I was going pretty well I think for a beginner but on the third lap something broke in the timing gear and that was that."

The Zenith was, of course, a vee-twin J.A.P. so this experience served to confirm G.B.'s preference for the type. Already widely experienced as a motorcyclist and tuner, G.B. added greatly to his store of knowledge during the first world war when he was employed on war work at the White and Poppe engine works at Coventry.

On essential work, he was allowed petrol and bought and tested all the machines he could get his hands on.

" Before I started to build my own machine I had owned and ridden 34 different makes and knew the good and bad points of

Ron Storey, works tester and sprint star (seated), and George Brough at Doncaster speed trials in 1926

them all . . . and I made a profit out of them as a rule," he said.

It was this "suck it and see" principle which introduced him to the Harley Davidson bottom-link fork which he was later to adopt in improved form for all his fast motors. "I remember going to Suffolk to collect my first Harley . . . I had not ridden five miles before I realized that this was the fork for a fast bike."

It was at Coventry, during the war years, that the first B.S. was born. Friends at the Montgomery motorcycle works helped with parts and No. 1 had a distinct Montgomery look about it. The engine was the 90 bore (90×77mm) J.A.P., a pre-war design but the biggest engine in production—and it did have overhead valves, albeit vertical ones. The gearbox was a three-speed Sturmey Archer, made in Nottingham, and there was all-chain drive with an Enfield cush hub at a time when the diehards maintained that the chain would never oust the belt. The original press report stated that the engine and gearbox were specially designed for Mr. Brough . . . certainly they were modified in detail and "Show" finished and there were a number of refinements which were to appear on nearly all B.S. machines, such as finned exhaust port attachments and brazed-in handlebars.

But the crowning glory was the B.S. tank, a shapely saddle tank with the bulbous nose of the type which was to grace every subsequent B.S., gleaming in nickel plate relieved only by a black panel on the top. Seen against the contemporary back-ground of flat tanks squeezed between frame top tubes, this tank was a crowd gatherer. Young G.B. brought the No. 1 machine back to Nottingham at the end of hostilities and it marked the point at which the policies of father and son diverged. W. E. Brough was committed to a flat-twin design of substantially pre-war styling and performance . . . a very fine effort from an engineering standpoint because it was built entirely in the Vernon Road works at Nottingham. Young George was equally set on the big solo vee-twin theme. The difference of opinion was too fundamental for compromise. G.B. had to go his own way. The announcement of his intention to produce his master-piece for sale . . . in the 25 November 1920 edition of *The Motor Cycle* . . . must have hit the motorcycle world with the impact of a bomb. There was no mention of price.

"Within 48 hours of that announcement I had received cheques from 20 enthusiasts who wanted one," he recalled. That first announcement would give a present-day advertising copy writer convulsions but there was no mistaking the message or the sincerity. Written in the idiom of the day, without flowery phrases, it was to start a 20 year run of highly personalized advertisements which forged a close link with enthusiasts throughout the world.

The magic name Brough Superior . . . who thought that one up? Not G.B., as a matter of fact. What to call the new bike was the subject of a discussion in a pub and the man in the corner—his name was Bob Blay—put down his pint and said "Why not call it a Brough Superior?" It was the obvious answer. The more printable part of what George's father said when he heard was "I suppose that makes my bike the Brough Inferior." "It wasn't meant like that at all," says G.B., "we had different ideas on what a motorcycle should be, that was all."

Just what G.B.'s idea of a motorcycle was is best outlined by what he wrote for *Motor Cycling* in 1924.

"I told myself that what was wanted was a big solo machine made up to an ideal and not down to a price : that it must have everything of the best in its manufacture and that it must start easily . . . there had been big sporting solos but the run and jump business was a thing of the past. So I decided that my machine must have a gearbox clutch, kickstarter and all-chain drive. I knew that the public did not want a machine which was virtually a sidecar model adapted for solo use by the fitting of a higher gear. I knew they wanted a machine designed from the experienced solo rider's point of view. I was told it was madness to make a high-priced machine at a time when prices were falling and the public were demanding lighter and cheaper machines. I had my own convictions however : I thought there was a market, even with prices falling and slumps setting in, for an ultra-luxurious solo.

I knew the market was limited but I was not proposing to manufacture on the mass production scale. Each machine was to be a 'personal job' as one might say, carefully tested to see that it incorporated all those details that 'make the difference'. Results have proved I was right. The first Brough Superior was guaranteed to be capable of 8 to 80 miles per hour in top gear and it fulfilled its guarantee.

Just as a thoroughbred hunter appeals to a judge of good horse flesh so my machine was intended to appeal to the connoisseur motorcyclist. The chief fascination of riding a well-designed big twin is not so much the all out speed of which it is capable as the feeling of tremendous reserve power always at one's command. Critics say 'What is the use of having a machine which will do 80 m.p.h. when there are scarcely any roads on which this speed can be attained ?' The answer is that 50 m.p.h. on a machine which will only do 55 m.p.h. is very tiring. Everything seemed to be buzzing and hurrying, and to one who is used to the rhythm of a big twin merely purring along at a similar speed it seems that a lot of unnecessary fuss is being made to say nothing of the difference in comfort due to the absence of vibration in the larger machine.

Again the freshness of the rider of the big twin is also reflected in the machine. It can do 80 m.p.h. and consequently when it is touring on a whiff of gas at 40 m.p.h. it is underworked. I honestly do not think that a big twin driven at 40 m.p.h. costs more to run than a three-fifty run at 40 m.p.h. The big bus has such an easy time that tyres, chains, gears and working parts of the engine will at this speed wear much longer than they will on a three-fifty maintaining the same speed."

G.B. set up shop in a single-storey factory in Haydn Road, Nottingham . . . the building was unique in its day, being made of concrete on an early prefab principle . . . and a hectic period began. All the early B.S. machines were built on the bespoke system like a Savile Row suit. A visit to the works and a chat with the maker was almost obligatory. That discussion would cover the use to which the machine would be put, the rider's fads and fancies, and his size, for each machine was "tailored" as to riding position. No Brough ever had such common expedients as an adjustable handlebar. The bar was shaped to suit the purchaser and brazed in position. (A feature which a small chap like me always found a trifle uncomfortable.)

In view of the limited finances of the firm a substantial deposit was more or less obligatory, too. In the early days G.B. was chief salesman and tester rolled into one. Later as production

soared to two or three machines a week, a likely lad, Ron Storey, was taken on as tester. He became the star "works rider" when G.B. retired from speed events to placate his family. Their alarm was occasioned by his 100 m.p.h. crash at Clipstone Drive in 1923 when "Old Bill," his side-valve sprinter, crossed the finishing line to make f.t.d. but without G.B. in the saddle.

To Haydn Road came indefatigable Ike Webb, ex-Grenadier Guards and Royal Marines, who was to have a hand in the making of every production Brough Superior. He had lived next door to the Brough family when a boy.

Ike made friends and satisfied customers of B.S. owners throughout the world . . . with princes and poets and Lawrence of Arabia, no less. Great days when the constant search for perfection produced new models without thought of profit-making series production . . . development falling into a now familiar pattern. First an idea, then a G.A. drawing which would have to pass G.B.'s eye for line ("What looks right is right" was his motto) . . . the frenzied building of a prototype because he could not wait to try it, and then the traditional hard riding weekend over the Derbyshire roughery.

Those test runs were calculated to find the weak points in anything. Not always did G.B. turn up at the works on Monday with a smile. Sometimes there would be a phone call from the wilds and the Overland van would be dispatched to bring in the remains. It became a tradition that the new model would be "blooded" in one of the M.C.C. long-distance trials. That was how the first model had made its public debut in 1920. And of course there always had to be new surprise models at the Olympia Show. From the first, B.S. machines were successful in trials and speed trials and the circle of B.S. competition widened to include such famous men as Harold "Oily" Karslake, doyen of long-distance riders, Watson Bourne, H. B. Chantry, Charles Needham and speedmen like Freddy Dixon, Bert le Vack, E. C. Baragwanath, Joe Wright, George Patchett, Arthur Greenwood, Tommy Spann, etc.

Buying a B.S. was not so much the purchase of a machine but the initiation to an exclusive club of which G.B. was the Captain. Not only did the members add tremendously to the achievements of the marque, but because it was such an essentially matey affair they added materially to the development of the machine. But

Lawrence of Arabia . . . then Aircraftman Shaw . . . takes delivery of his last B.S. from the works. G.B. is on crutches as the result of a crash in the I.S.D.T. at Grenoble

Above : George Brough on "Old Bill" at Clipstone speed trials, 1922. Below : Same bike, sidecar attached, in semi-retirement at Stanford Hall, 1964

wise, was in 1933 when he nursed an ambition to win a Brooklands Gold Star for a lap at over 100 m.p.h. with a sidecar. If he had tackled the job as a professional rider with a proper track outfit he would undoubtedly have succeeded but he chose to go about it clubman style with an engine he had ridden in the Edinburgh Trial, a road-going sidecar and a 1927 frame. He missed the mark by 0.79 m.p.h. Bearing in mind that ace B.S. trackman Baragwanath never bettered 99 m.p.h. per lap with an unblown engine, and his blown record at that time was 103, it was nothing to be ashamed of.

What, you may ask, had this to do with the B.S. you could buy ? Everything. Could there have been a better way of improving the breed than for the maker to be the chief tester extraordinary ? The practical dividends were endless. Foremost was the fact that every B.S. steered as if on rails. Thanks mainly to the Harley inspired fork, there was never a Brough Superior which did not inspire supreme confidence at maximum speed. The doubting Thomas could always have a " hands off at 100 m.p.h." demonstration laid on by Ron Storey. This, at a time when the speed wobble was a characteristic of most other fast machines. Incidentally, the Brough Superior is the only machine in my experience that steers equally well with or without a sidecar . . . with no fork alteration. A detail which no other

although some of the club members were supreme in their own particular competition sphere G.B., as behoves a Captain, retained the title of the best all-rounder. In sprints he took f.t.d. 51 times out of 52 events (the 52nd was that aforementioned mishap at Clipstone), in M.C.C. events he won premier awards 23 times out of 24 occasions. He won races at Brooklands and took f.t.d. in Alpine hill climbs (hence the famous type name Alpine Grand Sports) and was a regular rider in the early I.S.D.T.s.

In 1928 he held the honour of having travelled faster on two wheels than anyone . . . 130.6 at Arpajon. If one piston had not collapsed on the return run it would have been a world record. Next year he lent the bike to Bert Le Vack who completed the two-way attempt and took the record. G.B.'s final fling, speed-

designer has mastered.

Because the maker spoke from experience . . . sometimes hard experience . . . no one was more ruthless in his demands to the manufacturers of his components. There was, for instance, the matter of the gearboxes which failed to keep pace with the development of bigger and better B.S. engines. After a particularly bad attack of gearbox busting, G.B. loaded the van with specimens and went round to Sturmey Archers himself. Button-holing the S.A. boss, Sir Harold Bowden, he argued that instead of having to build his bikes down to their gearbox they ought to build their box up to his bike. They did : the outcome was the S.B. (special Brough) box, a scaled-up version fitted to the more hirsute Broughs.

Outside the Haydn Road works in 1926. George Brough is giving a send-off to Eddy Meyer, Austrian Brough agent and national record-holder. On Meyer's left are Ike Webb, Harold " Oily " Karslake and Bill Smith, the works clerk. In the background, G.B.'s personal Alpine Grand Sports

Right from the earliest days the overriding policy had been " Only the best is good enough." Manufacturers of components had a very rough time at the hands of the rider-manufacturer. Anything which did not come up to the exacting standard demanded went back . . . sharpish. Bearing in mind that the quantities bought by G.B. were hardly enough to form a sales manager's dream, and the special finishes and detail modifications demanded could seldom have been a sound commercial proposition, it speaks highly for B.S. diplomacy that the parts were supplied at all. The truth was, perhaps, that all the suppliers were proud to be associated with this two-wheeled status symbol and wrote off any losses as advertising and prestige.

Engines were bought " ready to run " and were immediately fitted to the frame. Test showed whether they were up to scratch . . . the B.S. road test was a real test, not a round-the-houses potter. Many were the engines which had to be stripped down because of excessive noise, low performance or piston seizure. If the causes could not be eradicated by selective assembly or hand fitting, the engine would be packed in a box and sent back to the maker.

If the production standard was high, the Show standard was out of this world. Show-wise, G.B. had a reputation as a crowd stealer. Superhuman efforts were made to prepare the one-off models. Even when it was a race against time, the standard was never relaxed.

There was the time when a prototype was being finished off with only a few hours to go before the Show deadline. G.B. came down to the erecting shop to inspect the masterpiece. " That tank," he said, " there's something wrong with the lines of it. You'll have to make another." " Impossible. There's no time," argued the staff. Tanks, of course, were the most specialized part of the machine, being soldered up from innumerable hand-beaten sections. G.B. did not waste time arguing. Picking up a hammer from the bench he stove in the one and only Show tank. " Now you will have to make a new tank," he said. They did.

The changeover from J.A.P. engines to Matchless in the early '30s (only the 11.50 model continued with the J.A.P. engine) came about because J.A.P.s were no longer prepared to modify their engines to keep pace with G.B.'s search for perfection. The J.A.P. engine was essentially vintage in design, and although the performance was there it gradually fell short of the demand for performance-with-refinement. It was a trifle rough, rather noisy and somewhat messy. On the other hand, Matchless, who had reached a higher standard of refinement, were looking for markets for their engines and were willing to lean over backwards to gain the plum contract .. from a prestige point of view. Experiments started with the side-valve 1,000 c.c. engine . . . not all plain sailing, for the engine which powered Matchless motorcycles was found wanting when Brough testers got to work on it.

The side-by-side connecting rods rattled at certain speeds, the special low-expansion close-fitting pistons seized when driven hard . . . but the Matchless engineers fitted forked rods and got over the piston trouble : most of it was due to unequal distortion under heat caused by the cast-in valve chest. Truncating this valve chest to let cooling air get round the valve pockets overcame the trouble. After the side-valve came the o.h.v. 1,000 c.c. MX engine with hairpin springs which gave approximately the same performance as a normal J.A.P. (as distinct from a racing version) with greatly improved quietness, slow running and wearing qualities.

There were a host of details which owed their place to the fact that G.B. was the most critical user of B.S. machines. The prop stand (" Oily " Karslake designed this), the optional pannier cases (the outcome of G.B.'s Alpine touring), finger brake adjustment, hinged rear mudguard, dipping headlamps, twin interconnected silencers (to give an even exhaust note), flyscreens, twin headlamps, crash bars, legshields. All these refinements were pioneered, many of them passing into common usage on other makes.

Surveying what you might regard as the extra-mural activites of G.B. and his merry men in competitions, I marvel that they ever produced machines for the man in the street at all. As a schoolboy, living no more than half a mile from the Haydn Road works, I hung about for hours in the hope of seeing one of the testers set out. I could never quite understand why there were no obvious signs of activity . . . no roar of machinery and thud of ponderous presses. I can understand it now, realizing that most of the parts were bought out.

But the records show that, one-offs apart, they produced some 3,000 machines in the 20 years of production. Longest run was the 986 c.c. J.A.P.-engined SS80 from 1923 to 1932 with a total of 624 machines, next best the o.h.v. 680 c.c. J.A.P. model from 1926 to 1933 with 547, next the Matchless-engined SS80 from 1933 to 1939 with 460. The prestige model SS100 ran to 281 machines with J.A.P. engines from 1925 to 1935, and with Matchless engines up to 1939 with a total of 102. The 11.50 J.A.P. model, sold widely for police work, from 1933 ran to 308. No records are available for the early Mk. 1 models of 1920 and early 1921 with 90 bore J.A.P. units, but 137 similar machines were made with side-valve J.A.P.s.

The Mk. II model, which was the same machine fitted with the 6 h.p. i.o.e. M.A.G. engine, must have been an instant success for over 200 were produced. A side-valve 680 was made chiefly for export to Austria around 1927 and although no records are available it is thought that over 200 were made. But an attempt in 1932 to market a popular-price Brough by fitting a 680 c.c. side-valve J.A.P. in the old Mk. I type frame was a resounding flop. Only 10 were made. The dealers who asked for it were wrong ! Other models which did not really get off the ground for various reasons were the o.h.v. 500 of which nine were made and three are still in existence, the 750 c.c. side-valve J.A.P. . . . a smaller-engined edition of the 1927 SS80 . . . and the o.h.v. 750, a bigger-engined 680. And of course the Austin Seven-engined, twin rear wheel machine which was the biggest Show sensation of all time . . . and still is the best crowd gatherer. So many different stories are told of the numbers produced that it is high time the truth was told. Ten Austin fours were made and such is the high survival rate of unusual machines that at least four are

still running. From what I gather of the story of the Austin four, the real achievement was not so much in installing it in a machine but in the diplomacy with which G.B. persuaded Sir Herbert Austin to supply the engines.

The last occasion when G.B.'s itching twistgrip hand persuaded him to plan a real road burner was in 1932 when there was a plan to revive the Sidecar T.T. for 1933. The plan flopped because a trade faction believed the sight of sidecar outfits dicing crazily with wheels in the air and passengers performing acrobatics would be death to the sidecar market rather than a fillip.

The practical result of G.B.'s enthusiasm was a banking sidecar and the fabulous (on paper anyway) " two of everything " SS100 J.A.P. The sidecar was G.B.'s variation on the original Fred Dixon banking sidecar theme which scored a runaway win in the 1923 Tourist Trophy. Whereas the Dixon device relied on almost telepathic understanding between rider and passenger . . . and a very muscular passenger at that because he had to overcome gravity and centrifugal force by hauling on the lever which raised or lowered the sidecar . . . G.B. contrived a device which produced the same result but without the passenger's assistance. This one-off, which is one of my prized possessions,

" And of course the Austin Seven-engined, twin rear wheel machine which was the biggest Show sensation of all time . . . ."

was destined for the T.T. that never was but finished up as a working exhibit at Olympia.

The SS100 for which it was intended was on paper the most outstanding machine since the original SS100. The engine rated at 8/75, compared with the previous 8/50, and was of very advanced design with deeply spigoted cylinder barrels, high camshafts, down-draught inlet ports angled for twin carburettors and twin bevel-driven magnetos (production ones had one Magdyno and one magneto).

A new frame permitted a pivot-mounted gearbox, and the whole ensemble was quite the most beautifully laid out Brough ever. Alas, it was not a success. The engine needed a lot more development and gave trouble on test. Six machines were built in 1934 and one in 1935 and the J.A.P. engine was then dropped in favour of the Matchless. Mind you, if the Sidecar T.T. had come off, or there had been a revival of interest in 1,000 c.c. racing to tickle G.B.'s fancy, I feel sure that development would have been continued to a point when the engine was right. Incidentally, when the model was announced the maker offered a money-back guarantee that it would reach and hold 110 m.p.h. solo and 90 with a chair. I do not know whether anyone of the seven buyers took him up on it. This two-of-everything model was listed at the traditional price for SS100 models of £170—

A rare one, this—the overhead-valve five-hundred . . ." of which nine were made and three are still in existence "

the price of the first SS100 and every one in between . . . you might say that G.B. was the original exponent of retail price maintenance.

Thereafter G.B. ceased to worship at the altar of pure speed and planned his magnum opus . . . the Dream four-cylinder which was to stagger the world. The only trouble was that Hitler had the same idea at around the same time, with the result that the Dream remained a dream as far as the buying public was concerned and will remain so for all time.

Certainly the design—two flat twins built one atop the other with geared crankshafts (to give theoretically perfect balance), unit gearbox and shaft drive—was the most advanced ever proposed. Imagine a B.M.W. with an extra engine built on top of the normal one and you have a pretty good idea of what it looked like . . . and if it had been developed to the perfection of two B.M.W.s you can imagine what it would have gone like. But it was a costly final chapter to the pre-war story of the B.S. and although further development was carried out after the war the plot was finally abandoned.

" Fours cost me a fortune one way and another and the Dream was the most costly of all, but I always had this ambition to build a world beater and I knew that all things being equal a good four would beat a good twin. History seems to have proved me right.

I wanted to go on with the Dream after the war but it was so complex that it would have absorbed all our production facilities. Materials were controlled and one had to undertake to export most of one's production. I could see also that the roads would get too crowded for big machines. It was hard to decide against making motorcycles but I had to think of my men . . . most of them had been with me for the whole of their working life and I just could not take the risk. The Brough Superior name lives on but it now stands for the highest quality in precision engineering."

As events have turned out in the motorcycle industry, there is no doubt that G.B. made the right decision. The market for

the connoisseur's 1,000 c.c. machine has dwindled to the point when no one can afford to make them. The wealthy parent no longer bribes his son through this finals with the promise of a B.S. . . . nowadays it has to be a sports car. The young enthusiast no longer wants a long-distance cruiser . . . he prefers something as near to a racer as he can get.

But although the motorcycle story ended with a dream which never came true, the war gave the B.S. team a chance to show what they could do to win the battle of war-time production.

In October 1939 the little band of 19 men left the Haydn Road works and moved to the Vernon Road factory of W. E. Brough which had been running as a machine shop after the Brough motorcycle had gone out of production in 1925. Before the month was through they had their first M.O.S. contract rolling out. Before the end of hostilities the labour force had grown to 333 working round the clock. An amusing twist of fate was that they were mainly employed on work for Rolls-Royce . . . the B.S. works was one of the few contractors entrusted with the job of machining Merlin crankshafts. Superhuman feats of precision and production were achieved by the men who had built B.S. motorcycles . . . Ike Webb being awarded the B.E.M. for his outstanding efforts as works manager.

So the Brough Superior motorcycle story ended on a symbolic note. The golden boy of a golden age of motorcycling finally built his dream bike . . . finished in gold at that, and with an odd twist of fortune's wheel it now rests on the very site on which the story began. And the craftsman's son now carries on the engineering tradition of his father.

His favourite machines ? Without a doubt the earlier SS100 and Alpine Grand Sports models and in later years the 11.50 model. He was never very interested in the 680 models. " I made the 680 because my dealer friends, Blackie (E. O. Blacknell of Nottingham who rode a specially prepared side-valve 680 in trials) in particular, pressed me to make a lower-priced machine they could sell in quantity but I was never very keen on them myself."

If still in doubt about the superiority of the Brough Superior you may ask yourself these questions. Where else could you buy machines to suit the individual taste? An Indian potentate had one silver plated from stem to stern. Other customers (strange ones, surely) had Broughs finished in special colours. Lawrence, as short in the leg as I am, had a 19in rear wheel instead of the normal 21in. A disabled Cheshire customer had an SS100 specially fitted with a self starter.

Where else could you get a potential world record machine run up for you? As did Joe Wright, Le Vack, Alan Bruce and Arthur Simcock, Eric Fernihough and Noel Pope. Where else in the vintage days anyway could you buy a machine with steering which had been tested up to 130 m.p.h.?

And today when, let's face it, motorcycles are rather demode, what machine still commands instant respect wherever you go ... that would be suitable for a visit to a doctor, a broker or a bishop? There is today perhaps one modern machine which would fill this bill but alas it is not made in this country.

Just as there have been countless legends about Rolls-Royce service ... you have heard the one about the owner who broke a half shaft on the continent, had it replaced by an R.-R. man flown out especially, and was told afterwards when he asked for the bill that the incident could not have happened because R.-R. half shafts did not break? ... so there are countless tales told about Brough Superior service.

Most of them feature Ike Webb and his brother Don who until his death three years ago looked after the repairs side. Always most grateful for the service was Lawrence of Arabia, who had a habit of turning up for a quick tune up before some marathon ride. The story I like best about Lawrence and his lone rides began when he collected a new SS100 from the works at midday on a Saturday. When Ike arrived for work on Monday ... and it would be before 8 a.m. rather than after if you knew Ike ... Lawrence was waiting on the doorstep with 1,000 miles on the clock and all the tread gone off the back tyre.

There was the son of a wealthy Scottish nobleman who against parental orders had been riding in sand races at Skegness, had broken off his exhaust port and had to get back home. He knocked Ike up at midnight, the two of them rode from the railway station to the works with the front cylinder making a noise like a Gatling gun. New parts were fitted, the tanks topped up and the youngster set off for Scotland. Ike went back to bed at 5.30 a.m.

Two legends of B.S. lore have been handed down to posterity by enthusiasts the world over and have been somewhat distorted in the process ... now at last I have been privileged to hear the story from G.B. himself.

First the classic slogan, " The Rolls-Royce of Motor Cycles," vide *The Motor Cycle*. How did G.B. win that priceless accolade? Well the words in question were written in 1924 by Mr. Teage, then Midland Editor of *The Motor Cycle*, in a road test report of an SS80. Stuck no doubt for words adequately to describe what was the most superior machine of the day, he did what you or I would do ... used the magic name as a superlative. G.B., always the publicity man, immediately used it in all advertisements and catalogues, always careful to attribute it to *The Motor Cycle*. All went well until one day a Rolls-Royce stopped outside the Haydn Road works and a V.I.P. from R.-R. was ushered into G.B.'s office.

Was Mr. Brough aware, the visitor asked, that he had been infringing the copyright of the R.-R. trade mark? Mr. Brough countered that he was only quoting what had been published. " No matter," the V.I.P. declared, " it is still an infringement."

Had the visitor ever seen a Brough Superior, asked Mr. Brough, trying to shift the conversation on to his own ground. No, but the visitor would like to. What he saw in the works was a batch of Show machines being prepared ... the fitters wearing white gloves to avoid finger marks on the pristine parts.

Brough Superior Dream

Brough Superior prototypes, one-offs and specials . . .

The final, most ambitious of all George Brough's projects—the flat-four Dream . . " so much promise . . such a costly disappointment . . "

Prototypes, one-offs and specials are usually more interesting to the historian than the bread and butter production models because they provide a deeper insight into the aims and ideals of the designer. It is particularly true of the Brough Superior, where for the whole of the period under review George Brough was supreme head of the firm. As I suggested in the previous instalment last month, he was producing machines for his own pleasure in the first place, for his riding friends in the second place, and if there was a third object it was that as many enthusiasts as possible of the same way of thinking as himself should be given an opportunity to ride a B.S. He was in the happy and almost unique position of not having to satisfy a board of directors.

The " one-offs," therefore, are as true an expression of the master as a signed painting by an artist.

The " collection " begins with Old Bill (derivation—Bruce Bairnsfather's immortal First World War " Tommy "), the side-valve sprinter which blasted G. B. to fastest time of the day 51 times out of 52 in a row between 1922 and 1923. Of the 52nd event more anon. Old Bill was not the first B.S. to be raced, for early in 1922 G. B. had taken a tuned, " show-finished " J.A.P.-engined Mk. 1 to Brooklands and had won a five-lap experts' scratch race on it before a tyre-burst curbed his enthusiasm for the track.

And even before that he had competed in sprints on a tuned

but near-standard 90 bore Mk. 1. This was fast but slow off the mark. It managed f.t.d. a few times but was beaten on short courses by smaller, lighter machines . . . Ernie Searle's three-fifty Sheffield Henderson for one.

But Old Bill was the first B.S. to be built as a racer pure and simple with sprints as the object in mind. And following the B.S. pattern of development, it was to be the prototype of a sporting line to be known as the SS 80.

The frame was a simple diamond, like the previous tourers, but lower around the saddle position . . . the sort of frame which other manufacturers were using for three-fifty side-valves. To cope with the torque of a lusty thousand motor, external bracing struts were fitted where they would do most good. Across the front engine plates ran a long bolt with distance pieces . . . some 18in long . . . and from this straight tubes ran back to the rear fork ends with another pair running up to the saddle lug. This triangulation effectively kept the rear wheel in line with the engine when some 30 hairy horses were liberated. Front forks were Brampton parallel-ruler type but the characteristic Brampton Biflex sprung top link was discarded in favour of a solid link. Wheels were 28×3in, beaded edge, the rear brake a dummy belt rim, the front a 5in Webb, the type on which the brake shoes are retracted by a huge circlip and which is about as effective a means of retardation as a prayer mat.

The gear box was a normal three-speed Sturmey Archer with a long gear lever mounted on the saddle tube . . . G. B. had a changing technique all his own which involved hooking the knob in the crook of his knee. The tank lying between the twin frame top rails was the only B.S. tank which was not of saddle type.

The engine was of course the *pièce de résistance*. I do not suppose his rivals knew at the time because externally it looked a perfectly normal early four-cam 85 × 85.5mm J.A.P. but it was in fact Bert Le Vack's works prototype motor. Actually Le Vack, as development engineer for J.A.P.s, had built a similar engine with a long stroke ratio (this one being subsequently raced by Baragwanath) but the square one was chosen for production and listed as 8/30 sports . . . the 30 stood for 30 b.h.p. It could propel a touring machine at 80 m.p.h. The unit was very much like the production engine . . . at least until G. B. and his merry men got to work on it . . . but the timing gear was more substantial.

Tuning followed the traditions of the day. The compression ratio was raised by machining the alloy fir-cone valve caps until they only just cleared the valves and when this did not achieve the desired result the crankcase mouths were machined down $\frac{1}{16}$ in to lower the cylinder barrels. The ports were opened out and polished, tulip inlets fitted with lightened collars and double springs, and carburation provided by a Binks Mousetrap. The standard J.A.P. flywheels, which resembled nothing so much as a couple of mill stones, were replaced by a G. B. set which were . . . and are, for they are still there . . . things of wonder. Machined from steel blanks, they are no more than a skeleton . . . a narrow rim with one diametrical " spoke " which carries crankpin and main shaft. The rest is daylight where the surplus metal has been cut away.

THE REAL POWER

All this contributed to the liveliness but the real power . . . and it was, in my opinion, the most potent side-valve ever produced in this country . . . comes from the timing.

The cams have large " lumps " which give a timing something like this . . .
    Rear cylinder :   Inlet opens 35 degrees, closes 65 degrees;
                             Exhaust opens 85 degrees, closes 30 degrees.
    Front cylinder :   Inlet opens 25 degrees, closes 65 degrees;
                             Exhaust opens 85 degrees, closes 40 degrees.
    Similar figures for the standard 8/30 engine are . . .
                             Inlet opens 15 degrees, closes 60 degrees;
                             Exhaust opens 62 degrees, closes 22 degrees.
Both cylinders being timed the same.

The increase in overlap from 37 degrees as standard to 65 degrees . . . a " dirt " J.A.P. only has 78 degrees . . . shows that G. B. had either a very early understanding of cylinder filling or had been particularly painstaking in the suck-it-and-see method of tuning. The results were electric. It was unbeatable off the line, having extraordinary pick up, and was more than once clocked at over 100 m.p.h. In its hectic heyday, it trounced such experts as Fred Dixon, who had an eight-valve Harley, and the redoubtable I. P. Riddoch who had an o.h.v. 1,000 c.c. Blackburne with his own system of forced induction.

It was a needle match with Fred Dixon which proved to be Old Bill's swansong and very near curtains for G. B. The scene was Clipston Drive, home ground for G. B., a narrow drive to a private house with a loose surface of water-bound pebbles. With the finishing line in sight and Old Bill peaking at nearly the 100 mark, the beaded front tyre tore away from the security bolts and wrapped round the forks. Old Bill went over the line all right like a runaway projectile but G. B., who for once had come to the line without his leather jacket, did not get that far. The B.S. followers present claimed f.t.d. for the wreckage of the bike. Fred Dixon who had made next best time argued with some logic that " rider had to be on t'bike." G. B. in an ambulance on his painful way to hospital was in no position to argue. In fact he was not to see Old Bill again for many a long year . . . until 1959, in fact. How this came about is quite a story and because so many famous machines vanish without trace it is refreshing to tell of one that did not.

With the " boss " in hospital, every penny counted at the works and anyway the side-valve was soon to be superseded by

an o.h.v. J.A.P. that Bert Le Vack was putting the finishing touches to, so Old Bill was straightened out, fitted with a new pair of forks (that is why it now has extra-heavy Webbs) and disguised as a sports model with valanced mudguards and a standard tank.

When they dismantled it they found a solid wad of earth rammed up the rear exhaust pipe . . . rammed right up to the open exhaust valve as the bike slid along. It was sold to someone at Southport and next appeared in the showrooms of Messrs. Lifes of Southport, who advertised it as follows :

" Old Bill, Mr. Geo. Brough's personal side-valve 100 m.p.h. racer, like brand new, deliberate sacrifice, 92 guineas."

In June 1925 it suffered the indignity of being registered under the Roads Act as FR 3925. Type or Model was given as Sport, and where there should be a frame number is the frank admission " no number." After that the trail becomes confused but in the '30s it was owned by H. K. G. Garland who lived in Surrey and used it on the road and in the odd sprint at Gatwick and Brighton. It was Garland who fitted a later rear wheel with internal-expanding brake after the belt rim brake had torn all the spokes out when going down a steep hill.

He sold it to his friend Basil Budgett who hitched on a touring sidecar and used it for long-distance camping trips . . . until there was hardly a tooth left on a sprocket. Hitler's air raids then did their best to break the old warrior . . . the mews garage where it was garaged during the blitz was bombed and Old Bill was buried in rubble. To his everlasting credit, Budgett felt that Old Bill was not just any old bike and salvaged it. Years later, realizing that he would never get around to rebuilding it, he earned my life-long gratitude by writing to me out of the blue and offering it to me.

Rebuilding was a labour of love and the crowning joy was when I was able to invite G. B. to ride Old Bill again and this time complete the course . . . because, believe it or not, Clipston Drive is still there, pebbles, potholes and all. We pushed him off . . . he shot away so smartly that I fell flat on my face, and disappeared in a cloud of dust.

Afterwards G. B. wrote thanking me. " I thoroughly enjoyed my reunion with my dear old pal Old Bill. You had prepared him marvellously and the old ' kick in the pants ' which you get when you turn up the wick was there ' as of yore '." (Can you think of any other manufacturer who would feel like that about one of his motorcycles ?)

OLD BILL'S RETIREMENT

Old Bill spends most of his time in the Stanford Park Museum these days and I have never attempted to tune for maximum power in deference to his years but he still has enough energy to have won the sidecar class at the V.M.C.C. Royston Hill Climb and to have recorded 18.6s for the standing quarter at Wellesbourne with a heavy sidecar passenger (F. P. H., to be exact).

In 1923 Brian Allen, the Allen of the Croydon firm of Allen-Bennett, one of the first Brough agents, persuaded G. B. to build him a replica of Old Bill. Outwardly the machines were alike as peas even to the bracing struts although Allen's machine had his own pet idea of a telescopic sprung saddle pillar. But the engine was obviously a production 8/30 and Allen did not achieve any fame with it.

The engine which Le Vack was " putting the finishing touches to " . . . the 8/45 . . . was a winner. In a spidery frame not unlike Old Bill's, but with Harley forks and a Brough saddle tank, he raised the world record to 119 at Arpajon in 1924, thereby inscribing Brough on the record annals for the first time . . . it was to appear on two more occasions.

Next works racer was the machine which was illustrated last month with Ron Storey up. Nowadays it would be termed a works development model for it was the prototype of the Pendine model.

From the moment the SS 100 model was introduced in 1924, private owners raced them with success wherever courses were suitable. Sand racing was the ideal medium. The works SS 100 was developed as a pukka racer and the experience gained was used in the production of the Pendine model, an over-the-counter 110 m.p.h. projectile sold to selected riders in 1926 and 1927.

Ron Storey cleaned up in the spot vacated by G. B., who had retired from the active list to placate his parents. Sometimes the works job was loaned to Arthur Greenwood who used it with a sidecar. From the works model stemmed the characteristic Pendine features of a petrol tank held down by steel straps, both exhaust pipes on the off side instead of cross-over pipes on the road jobs, a small Hartford friction damper in front of the steering head and the special heavyweight gear box. From the undisputed mastery of the model at the Welsh T.T. sand races at Pendine (Tommy Spann won four years running) came the type name Pendine . . . and G. B.'s house has been named Pendine ever since.

Behind one f.t.d. run by the works job at Southport is a tale of improvisation typical of B.S. teamsmanship. Starting up the engine after fitting some hush-hush ultra-light valves, Stan Greening of J.A.P.s blipped the throttle a mite too hard and a valve hit the piston, knocking the head sideways and breaking the guide. There were no spare valves, the position seemed hopeless and G. B. and Greening went off for breakfast disconsolate.

Ike Webb cajoled their toolroom wizard, Bruce Alvey, to do his best. Somehow the valve was straightened, a new guide turned up and when the head men returned the motor was as good as new . . . good enough to take f.t.d. anyway.

They were early risers, those B.S. men. Preparing for Doncaster speed trials, they would be away at dawn to put the bike through its paces over the course before anyone was about, and back the 45 miles to Nottingham before the works opened at eight.

RECORDS ON THE PENDINE

Two outstanding performances by Ron Storey on the " works development " Pendine deserve to go down in Brough history. One was his 122 m.p.h. record run at Saltburn Sands in 1928 and the other was at Brighton Speed Trials in 1932 when he duelled with Malcolm Campbell in a supercharged 4 litre Sunbeam and beat him.

The works bike was modified and remodified from time to time and it is difficult to follow its history but the frame was recently discovered at the works and is now being built up by Berk Milnes of Leicester.

Only one more works racer was built and that was the job built for G. B.'s attempt on the world's record at Arpajon in 1927. Fred Dixon helped with this project and when it first appeared there was an unmistakeable Dixon look about it . . . a gear lever like a railway signal lever pivoted on the front engine plates for one thing, and hush hush screening of the twin carburettors to fool the opposition for another. To suit Dixon's theories about handling, the front down tube was more upright, the engine further forward than normal and the gearbox was mounted on its side. I cannot really see that all this was necessary in view of the perfect handling of the standard frame.

Dixon had some bad luck with the machine at Brooklands, including a burst tyre crash when riding it solo, but he did win the Brooklands sidecar championship and G. B. got his ride at Arpajon when, if he did not get the record, he did (as related last month) gain the honour of having travelled faster one way than anyone else (130 m.p.h.). Bert le Vack took over the machine, removed a lot of the Dixon gimmicks and took the record next year. Thereafter it seems to have stood idle until in the '30s M. N. Mavrogordato bought it to realize an ambition of getting a Brooklands Gold Star . . . something he could not do with his

beloved Scotts. Still substantially original save for a later gearbox, it is now at Beaulieu.

Mind you, I think it was a bit naughty of G. B. to use a picture of this one-off in catalogues with the caption " Freddy Dixon on his Standard SS 100 Pendine Model."

Thereafter all the special racing Broughs were private-owner jobs . . . built by their owners but frequently with unstinting help from the works. First came Baragwanath's blown job in 1930. Its successes culminated with Noel Pope's all-time Brooklands lap records of 124 solo and 106 sidecar; and his gallant but unsuccessful attempt on the world record at Utah are too well known to be repeated here . . . and are worth an article on their own anyway.

STORY OF LEAPING LENA

Not so well known is the story of Leaping Lena, a private-venture attempt on the world sidecar record which succeeded on the second attempt at Tat in Hungary in 1932 when Alan Bruce clocked 135 m.p.h. Lena was built in 1931 by an Australian foursome, Arthur Simcock, Alan Bruce, K. Horton and Phil (Slide Rule) Irving. I think it is fair to describe the machine as inspired by Barry's Brough as it had the same set up of a No. 8 Powerplus supercharger slung in plates ahead of the engine.

The same lorry-type Amal fed the blower (changed next year for a larger No. 9 model) and the J.A.P. engine was of the same type as Barry's save for a twin-port head on the front pot. They, too, were troubled by unequal distribution of charge which had plagued Barry. The only real difference lay in the fact that they completely enclosed the works in streamlined panels and fitted a streamlined tail which faired off the rider's rump. He had a streamlined crash helmet too . . . the recognized wear for record aspirants in those days. The sidecar was a particularly fine piece of work; of slipper shape, it had the normal-size wheel completely enclosed. The quartet had a lot of bad luck, including a bit of suspected sabotage when someone dropped a foreign body into the blower works, and projected solo attempts had to be scrubbed.

What happened to Lena ? Quizzed on the subject, Phil Irving said it was dismantled and all the bits went back to the people they had been borrowed from.

Away in Austria the B.S. agents Eddy and Kent Mayer . . . Eddy was pictured last month . . . had been working on a similar project themselves. Again the basis was a Pendine model with an 8/50 J.A.P. but instead of the ponderous Powerplus blower used by Barry and Bruce (the Powerplus was a car unit designed to be mounted on the front of M.G.s, etc.) a locally produced unit with three geared rotors was used. It was only half the size of the British blower and in consequence could be installed in front of the engine without cranking the down tube. It was supposed to charge at 1.2 atmospheres when running at 6,000 r.p.m. and to demand an input of 8 h.p. for the privilege. The carburettor was a track type Amal instead of the now familiar " lorry " type.

Unfortunately the machine did not come up to its owners' expectations. They were aiming at the solo and sidecar world records and all they managed was an Austrian national record.

FERNIHOUGH'S RECORDS

All was quiet on the Brough record-breaking front for three years until a new name was added to the B.S. roll of honour— Eric Fernihough. Fernihough, who had done prodigious things with tiny engines, nursed a long-standing ambition to have a crack at the world's record, standing monotonously to the credit of Ernst Henne on a supercharged seven-fifty B.M.W. By way of preparation there was the Brooklands lap record to aim at.

His approach to the problem was original. Treating a big twin as two separate singles, he fitted a pair of speedway-type barrels and heads . . . each being capable of propelling a solo at over the ton . . . provided them with their own magnetos and

Originally built for George Brough's 130 m.p.h. outing at Arpajon, and also ridden by Fred Dixon at Brooklands, this vee-twin racer was afterwards taken over by Bert Le Vack for record-breaking

Close-up of the early SS 80; this one is actually a 1923 type, two-cam 980 c.c. J.A.P. and is still in the possession of its original owner, L. P. Peters

carburettors, and started the fashion of facing both exhaust ports forward, Vincent style. The choice of a frame was obvious. Only a B.S. steered well enough and only G. B. was likely to back such a project. In the first year of development, however, the B.S. looked rather un-B.S. like for Fernihough used Webb forks.

When Fernie began to lap the track at around 115 with half-mile bursts at 125 without the aid of a blower, Noel Pope, by this time custodian of Barry's blown Brough, decided it was time he put the record on a higher shelf . . . which he did at 120.59. Fernihough replied with a new record of 123 and then had Broughs fit a blower preparatory to his attack on Henne's latest figure, which was 169 in 1936 on a five-hundred B.M.W. Fernie was rubbing it in.

In 1937 Fernihough took the record by half a mile an hour in one of the most gallant lone record attempts ever. That was to be the last B.S. record (by this time Fernie had switched to Castle forks) and the last time Britain was to hold the record. Taruffi, 492 c.c. Gilera, added 1 m.p.h., and Henne finally raised it to 173½ before the year was out. Tragically, Fernihough tried again next year and was killed. The remains of the Brough were sold piecemeal.

To complete this chapter of speed Pope fitted an 8/80 type J.A.P. . . . a production racing engine based on Fernihough's home-built one . . . and before Brooklands closed for ever set an all-time high of 124.5 m.p.h.

From a trials point of view, the days of the B.S. were numbered when long-distance road trials gave way to sporting mud plugs. G. B. upheld his reputation in the M.C.C. events but always with same-as-you-could-buy models . . . he was just not interested in machines built solely for mud.

Two B.S. stalwarts did build specials to keep the B.S. flag flying. One was Freddy Stevenson, a Bulwell garage proprietor who had been in at the B.S. story right from the start. When the opposition from short-wheelbase lightweight trials outfits got too hot in 1934, he built a sidecar wheel-drive job by cutting the back end of his J.A.P. SS 80 and fitting a back axle with Austin Seven wheels. This had power and traction . . . so much so that one day the front wheel bogged down and the back wheels kept on pushing until the front forks folded back.

Solo mud plug exponent was E. O. " Blackie " Blacknell, the Nottingham dealer, who built a cut and shut side-valve 680 for the job.

Three other specials deserve mention, not because they really fit into B.S. history but because they were and still are talked of with awe when Brough enthusiasts meet. They had one thing in common . . . they were both larger than life as Broughs went. The first was the Karbro Express, a monster built by Harold Karslake . . . " Oily " for short. Harold, as one of G. B.'s earliest cronies, had the key of the door as far as the B.S. works went and managed to stretch one of the old 90 bore J.A.P. engines to nigh on 1,500 c.c. The object was torque at low speeds and with a compression ratio around 4 to 1 it was firing at every telegraph pole on a 2.75 to 1 top gear. The rest of the machine was basically Mk. 1 stretched a bit to make room for the oversize engine . . . " Oily " was long in the leg, which was just as well.

MOBY DICK: 106 IN SECOND

The other monster was Moby Dick, and the way it has got itself photographed over the years illustrates the advantage of having a catchy nickname. It started life as a standard spring-frame SS 100 of 1929 bought by Charles Hobbs of Guildford and became his absorbing hobby in the early '30s. The capacity was increased to 1,200 c.c. by, I suspect, using the 85mm bore of the 8/45 engine on the long-stroke 8/50 crankcase. Twin carburettors, high-compression pistons—the lot—were added from time to time, and with Brooklands cans on, Moby Dick certainly looked an eyeful. Dennis May, " Castor " of *Motor Cycling* in those days, appears to have made an annual event of road testing it and claimed 106 in second and 120 in top. It was not all bally hoo either for it won solo and sidecar classes at Gatwick speed trials in 1931 and shone in Brooklands M.C.C. high-speed trials. And it is still on the road in the hands of Tom Eccles of Burnley.

Record for the highest mileage probably goes to AU 7364, Ike Webb's one and only B.S., with a genuine one-owner mileage of 175,000 miles. It is a strong claimant, too, for the title of the most successful in *concours* events and for most modifications. And it was made entirely from discarded parts . . . beginning with a Mk. 1 frame which a customer bent in Madagascar and returned to the works for exchange, a Mk. 2 M.A.G. engine, Montgomery forks and a repaired Sturmey gearbox.

Over the years it was brought up to date as and when surplus bits came to hand. A two-valve J.A.P. engine replaced the M.A.G., Webb forks and wired-rim wheels replaced the early components. Barrels and heads from an 11.50 were grafted on to the crankcase, the cams modified to 8/30 contours. The final sidecar was the experimental B.S. loop chassis. Always immaculate, it won every *concours* event for which it was entered . . . winning the Watsonian Rally so regularly the organizers made him a judge to give future entrants a chance.

Sad to relate, it was sold soon after Ike left the B.S. works to become works manager of Blacknell Sidecars and in a few years became a rusty wreck. The latest news is that it has a new owner who is rebuilding it.

I do not know which heading covers my banking sidecar which, as explained last month, was to have been G. B.'s trump card

if the Sidecar T.T. had been held in 1933. Intended for racing, it was used in road trials and as an attraction at the Motorcycle Show. It is difficult to describe without drawings but the sidecar wheel is on a pivoted arm like the Dixon banking sidecar and when a locking pin is withdrawn by a foot pedal the arm allows the body and chassis to drop about 4in (it only banks to the left), to the dismay of unsuspecting passengers. Raising the body again to the horizontal is the cunning bit. A roller engages with a scroll attached to the sidecar wheel (the scroll is like a gramophone record with the shortest play ever) and rotation of the wheel . . . four turns actually . . . winds the body up again. Oh well, you must see it for yourself. G. B. told me that he got the idea from a lathe chuck.

That rounds up the specials built for a particular job and it leaves the specials which were built in search of an illusive ideal . . . in search of the intangibles of superiority.

THE FIRST FOUR

The first four, the 9 94 c.c. vee-four of 1927, was a staggering achievement for the Brough Superior works for it was all home made. The engine was in unit with a car-type clutch and gearbox with a final bevel drive to the final-drive sprocket. The dynamo for the coil ignition set was mounted almost vertically at the rear and driven from the gearbox. The four separate side-valve cylinders were mounted with the valves inside the V with an included angle of 60 degrees. A single camshaft ran at the bottom of the V. Tappet adjustment was made by inserting shims under the detachable tappet caps . . . a screw adjustment being out of the question in such a confined space. The carburettor was mounted on the off side of the crankcase, feeding through a duct to separate pipes inside the V. The outward result was an extremely clean unit but the fetish for symmetry and freedom from excrescences was, in light of present knowledge, one reason for its failure.

With the crank throws at the angle of the cylinders, running was uneven and carburation uncertain . . . today two carburettors would be considered obligatory with this layout. Another crankshaft was made to give even firing but vibration problems followed. With both layouts overheating was a problem . . . partly because of the distribution difficulties with one carburettor but mostly, I imagine, because of the hot spot between the two banks of cylinders.

But if it was a disappointment on the road it caused a furore at the Olympia Show. Displayed in a glass case (against show rules but a G. B. *fait au complait* on opening day), it took five policemen (real, not the commissionaire sort) at 5s per hour to keep the crowds back. Wags without the wherewithal to buy one anyway asked how one adjusted the well-nigh invisible tappets . . . G. B. remembered that taunt next year !

Colonel Tom Loughborough, who was manager of the Show, surveyed the crowds milling round a machine which was not for sale and said " George, you are a showman." " What do you . . . think I come here for," retorted G. B.

Next year G. B. was back with another four. He had talked Bert Le Vack, then development engineer at M.A.G. of Switzerland, into designing a straight four of 900 c.c. It was a car-type unit again, with unit clutch, four-speed box and final bevel, side valves on the off side and a quickly detachable tappet cover. At the Show a bold sign stated " Adjust tappets here." To gild the lily a new spring frame was built for it and twin headlamps, legshields, footboards and panniers thrown in for good measure. It was easily the most eyeable B.S. ever.

G. B. set off to test it in the Swiss mountains but, alas, it had a tendency to seize on the rear cylinders . . . again modern know-how in carburation and metals would have solved such problems. Given time, no doubt Le Vack would have got it right but tragedy intervened. Le Vack was killed in a road accident and with him the heart went out of G. B. and the

A " staggering achievement . . . for it was all home made " : the 1927 vee-four of 994 c.c. The separate side-valve cylinders had valves in the "vee"

The 1929 straight-four with car-style unit construction of engine, clutch, four-speed box and final bevel . . . and twin headlamps !

M.A.G. concern. But it was, I am told by those who rode it, a superb machine to ride, smooth, silent and supremely comfortable. And seizure of a four was no disgrace in those days. The works bought Henderson and American Ace fours for test purposes and seized them all.

Although the very thought is enough to make a B.S. addict blanch, there nearly was a B.S. two-stroke in the late '20s. Villiers came up with an experimental twin of approximately 500 c.c. . . . two pots on a common crankcase with a flywheel on one side and a flywheel magneto on the other . . . not to be confused with the 344 c.c. unit construction gearbox unit used by Francis Barnett in 1927. It was fitted in a bolted-up frame with the cylinders inclined forward with chain drive to a normal

gearbox. But it did not tick over like a Brough or go like a Brough and the project was dropped.

And though they do not like to talk about it there was in the same period a single-cylinder Brough with a 500 c.c. o.h.v. J.A.P. To add to the disgrace it did not steer like a B.S. and Ron Storey fell off it on test.

Despite two expensive disappointments, G. B. could not get the idea of a four out of his mind . . . it would be so smooth, so quiet, so easy to start, so much closer to the slogan of " The Rolls-Royce of Motorcycles." Why not, then, use a car engine suitably modified.

Only the Austin Seven unit was small enough, light enough to fit in a two-wheeler. An experimental job was run up in 1929.

No photographs have come to light but the layout was very like the M.A.G. four with a bevel box behind the gearbox and chain final drive. Ike Webb recalls trying in vain to solve the geometric problem of adapting the Austin gate change to foot change. The machine ran, was encouraging, and rumour says it was sold to an enthusiast in Derbyshire. It might have been the basis for a successful production series but G. B. had a better idea. There was at that time a fear, more imaginary than real perhaps, that the torque reaction of an in-line engine would spoil the steering of a solo. Pundits argued at length that an in-line engine would not work.

There was also a growing feeling that the machine of the future would have shaft drive. With one stroke of inventive genius, both birds could be killed with one stone. The plan was simple but outrageously unconventional. Only G. B. among manufacturers would have dared to attempt it. . . .

There would be two rear wheels just far enough apart to clear the drive shaft running between them. The machine would be perfectly balanced without any offset for the transmission line, transverse torque reaction would be absorbed in the twin wheels, and there would be the extra bonus of rear wheels as quickly detachable as on any car. Sir Herbert Austin was approached about engines and warmed to the project . . . the output of the standard engine (13 b.h.p.) was not considered enough for sidecar work so a sports version was agreed on . . . high-lift camshaft, high-compression alloy head (with *Brough Superior* cast on the side) and the cylinder bore taken to the maximum oversize to give 800 c.c. Apart from cooling difficulties, cured by fitting a water pump (there was not enough " head " for thermo syphoning), the project went smoothly.

G. B. made clear at the Show that for the time being it was only to be marketed as a sidecar outfit. It was possible to ride it solo . . . for this purpose the twin tyres were run soft so they would " give " when the machine was banked over. Hubert Chantrey, one of George's marathon riding pals, proved the point beyond question by taking one through the London-Exeter. E. O. Blacknell emphasized the point by riding one sitting backwards on the saddle.

One noticeable modification was made before more models were made . . . the prototype radiator with header tank blended into the familiar bulbous petrol tank was replaced with a more efficient and less costly radiator, more like a Scott.

But it was then that a completely unforeseen snag arose which caused further production to be abandoned. Taxation authorities ruled that with its four separate wheels the sidecar outfit was taxable as a car. In vain it was pointed out that the distance between the rear wheels was well within the limit laid down in Vehicle Construction and Use Regulations. Taxation authorities are a law unto themselves in such matters and while one tax office was amenable to reason on this point . . . it was so in Nottingham, not unnaturally . . . others were adamant.

By comparison, the transverse vee-twin of 1937 was almost ordinary. The Matchless side-valve engine from the current SS 80 was mounted transversely in a plunger spring frame modified by bifurcating the front down tube. To the driveside crankcase was bolted a car-type four-speed gearbox and clutch, and a bevel box took the drive out to the final chain. Enclosure of the works was one of the attractions. A bulbous oil tank covered the timing side of the crankcase and the Magdyno, driven now from behind the clutch, and the gearbox and bevel housing were completely enclosed in panel-beaten fairings.

The buying public was cagey, the fear of transverse torque reaction was still present, and the novelty was not considered worth the extra cost. The Show model was sold and is still believed to be running in Scotland. At the works the transverse twin was soon forgotten for the Dream was beginning to turn into reality.

Seldom if ever has a motorcycle design offered so much promise on paper as the Dream yet proved such a costly disappointment for reasons beyond the imagination or control of its sponsor. It can, as I have previously mentioned, best be imagined as two flat twins mounted one above the other with the crankshafts geared together and the drive taken from the lower one. The serpentine crankshaft and consequent couple of the normal flat-twin with two crank throws and pistons moving in opposition was obviated by running each " engine's " connecting rods on a common crankpin, one rod being forked. In consequence, the crankshafts were short and immensely rigid, being more truthfully two half shafts with integral crank cheeks, one formed with a 1⅜in crankpin to which the other cheek was bolted after the connecting rods had been assembled.

Gear rings bolted to the rear crank cheeks coupled the shafts, being " timed " so that all four pistons moved in the same direction at any time . . . all the theoretical implications of this unexpected feature are beyond me, though I can see that the out-of-balance forces of one " engine " would be cancelled out by its mate.

The dimensions of 71mm bore and 63mm stroke were surprisingly " over square " for the period, the alloy connecting rods, running direct on gudgeon and crankpin, impressively massive and very short. Cylinder blocks of light-alloy with pressed-in liners were topped each side with heads cast in one. The cylinder head and rocker gear layout can be conveniently likened to that of a Triumph twin, the resemblance being heightened by the fact that exhaust valves were operated by push rods in a tunnel at the front and inlets by a similar layout at the rear, where a single carburettor fed two inlets through a bolted on manifold.

The result was a most compact power pack . . . total width just over 20in. Developed to the performance of two Speed Twins on a common crankcase . . . and there was no basic reason why that yardstick should not have applied . . . there would have been over 50 smooth horses. With more to come, because the transverse layout offered ideal cooling . . . the heads and their hot exhausts in the perfect position to catch the breeze. Again using the Triumph twin yardstick, one can imagine a " hot " version producing enough power for a world-record breaker.

The rest of the machine was in keeping with G. B.'s avowed intention to produce the ideal motorcycle. Although the prototypes have a conventional gearbox . . . with positive-stop foot change and kick start, there was mention of a hush hush four-speed box so secret that it was never described, and a hand lever starter. Final drive was worm wheel and underslung worm to allow a low-level drive shaft. Accessibility had been studied. The rear wheel and drive could be detached from the plunger suspension in a couple of minutes. Detail work was superb.

G. B. had rallied his friends. Hatch, designer of the Mechanical Marvel Excelsior and Blackburne engines, was called in on the design side, Fred Dixon on the development side. Two machines were built, one finished in gold for the Show, the other in B.S. black and chrome for road test. The type name was " Dream ". It was the Show model that changed it to " Golden Dream " by common usage. Then the teething troubles began.

Carburation, with one port up draught and one down draught on each side, was uneven. When a single central carburettor was tried the long manifolds iced up. The only answer might have been four separate instruments. As the power was stepped up there was trouble with the connecting rods. Sudden seizures snapped the massive rods like carrots. Some said it was because the stroke was too short . . . too much angularity; the current success of the even shorter-stroke Ford car units suggests that it was not the geometry that was at fault. More likely it was the use of plain alloy connecting rods before the technique had been mastered. It is easy to be wise afterwards but a steel-lined big-end eye, a floating white-metal lined bush and a more positive pressure feed to the journals might have solved the problem. But flat fours are notoriously packed with gremlins. Jowetts were nearly driven round the bend before they tamed the Javelin, Nuffields planned a flat four for the Morris Minor but gave it up as a bad job . . . only the fanaticism of Hitler and the unlimited resources of a State project forced the VW engine through a lengthy labour. G. B. and his men only had months before the Hitler war called an abrupt halt.

Defeat the Dream project may have been, but not disgrace. One last attempt to make it tick was made in 1945. Another engine was built with four separate side-valve cylinders . . . side valves to permit a longer stroke while keeping the overall width down. There were more road tests but power was down, the sparkle gone.

The spirit of motorcycles lived on during the war years. There was a prototype A.R.P. fire pump outfit which had great possibilities. The pump unit was mounted on a special sidecar chassis with sidecar-wheel drive to make a highly manoeuvrable go-anywhere vehicle. The authorities hummed and hawed about the project and by the time they began to see its advantages it was too late . . . the works were too busy on work of higher priority.

In odd moments a Bradshaw-designed three-cylinder radial with disc valves was made up and tested with a propeller . . . this in 1942. The next year a similar engine was built with side valves and in 1944 Freddy Stevenson and Harold Karslake collaborated in the design of a big twin based on J.A.P. parts but of 90 degree angle. This gave more even firing but no worthwhile advantage on the road and was an awkward shape to fit in a frame.

Mystery surrounds the last experiment of all. A straight four engine was sent to Broughs for test. It was fitted to a frame and test ridden by Ron Storey . . . the test ending when the crankshaft snapped.

Always when dealing with the history of a *marque* one is asked for means of identifying models by year and type. With Brough Superiors this is no easy task because the constant quest for improvement plus the desire to please the individual customer confuses the trail. All one can say with certainty is that no two Broughs were ever identical for no two orders were the same. But there was, of course, a pattern based on catalogued models.

The pattern starts with models Mk. 1 and 2, the diamond-frame models based on the first ever and variously engined by J.A.P. and M.A.G., and a solitary Barr & Stroud. These models had exhaust pipes discharging into an expansion chamber in front of the engine with a long tail pipe, and detail changes were listed until 1924. They were joined in 1923 by the SS 80 which started life with a diamond frame like Old Bill but was rehoused in the cradle frame in 1924. This frame, the basis of all Broughs until 1931, was a masterpiece for it combined superb steering with a low centre of gravity and thoroughbred lines.

SS 80 models had the choice of two-cam sports or four-cam super sports side-valve engines (25 b.h.p. or 30 b.h.p.) and all had separate exhaust pipes and silencers. There were only detail changes until the model was given a new frame and re-engined by Matchless in 1933 but for 1929 a Bentley and Draper-designed pivoted fork spring frame was an optional extra for £10.

The introduction of the SS 100 model with Castle forks and sports exhaust system led to a popular variant . . . the made-to-order SS 80-100 as it was popularly called . . . actually a de-luxe 80 with the Castle forks and SS 100-type exhaust system (standard machines had the rear exhaust pipe taken under the gearbox to provide a balanced twin exhaust).

The SS 100 started in 1925 and for the first two years the exhaust pipes were high level, the front one taken round the down tube *via* a cast-aluminium finned adaptor. Oil was at first carried in a compartment of the petrol tank with sight feed

on top. In 1927 the SS 100 was listed in two forms . . . the road-going model was styled Alpine Grand Special (the result of G. B.'s success in the Alpine Trials) and the production racer version was called the Pendine (following sand-racing success at Pendine). The Pendine had both exhaust pipes on the offside, the strapped-down tank and narrow guards. In 1928 there was an engine change for the 100. The " square," 85.5 × 85mm o.h.v. J.A.P. was replaced by the long-stroke 80 × 99mm and the type name reverted to SS 100. A few racing versions called Pendine Specials were made to order. The super heavyweight gearbox became an option.

In 1929 the spring frame was offered on the SS 100 and this model may be regarded as the peak of development from a vintage point of view. The SS 100 remained virtually unchanged until a complete redesign in 1933 although a four-speed gearbox was introduced in 1932.

The o.h.v. 680 model was introduced in 1927 and was in all respects a scaled-down SS 100. The early engine was rather " cooking " with plain rocker bearings and primitive timing gear. The following year the engine was greatly improved, being a scaled-down version of the 8/45, and the machine was capable of 80 m.p.h. It was joined in 1930 by the Black Alpine model . . . finished in all black as the name suggested but with the added refinement of a four-speed gearbox . . . it cost £5 more. The spring frame became an option.

A 750 c.c. side-valve J.A.P. was offered in the 680 frame for 1928 only and 680 side-valves were made to order and for export but not listed.

Although only nine were made, the 500 c.c. overhead-valve model was catalogued for 1931 and it and its elder brother, the 680, were the first to appear with the new frame and pivotal gearbox which later was to become standard throughout the range. The new frame dispensed with the torque stays from gearbox mounting to rear wheel and was designed to take the latest Sturmey Archer gearbox which pivoted instead of sliding for adjustment. With dimensional differences it was used for all models from 1933 onwards . . . the nearest the B.S. ever got to standardization. With this frame came a first-rate cast-alloy primary oil bath divided horizontally so that one could renew the primary chain or attend to the clutch by removing four screws and without spilling any oil. It was into this frame that an oversize side-valve J.A.P. was fitted to launch the 11.50 model. The demand for a king-size side-valve came from the Canadian police who wanted a British machine to compete with the massive Harleys of their American colleagues across the border.

Personally, I regard the 11.50 as the epitome of the B.S. cult, combining the docility of a steam engine with the maximum of the roadburning o.h.v. models . . . the ability to go from 8 m.p.h. to 80 in top gear with a twist of the throttle. The bottom half of the engine was based on a heavy-duty motor which J.A.P.s had developed for the Morgan three-wheeler, having very robust timing gear which on the Morgan had to take the thrust of a starting handle.

Unlike all other J.A.P. twins, the cylinders on the 11.50 were set at 60 degrees instead of 50. This gave improved balance and incidentally made room in the V for a twin-carburettor induction pipe which was fitted to order. In 1933 the cylinders were similar to the old 8/30 engine though with detachable heads and the valve springs were exposed (apart from light-alloy dust covers). Alloy heads were tried but warped and were soon abandoned. This engine would rev to over 5,000 and turn out a comfortable 37 b.h.p. but its charm lay in the fact that it would produce some 25 b.h.p. at about half revs. But it was rather noisy mechanically and next year the cylinders were redesigned to enclose the valve springs and tappets in cast-in boxes. Quieter it was, but also heavier and prone to overheat. My preference remains for the early engine, noise or no noise. Until 1938 the

Magdyno was bevel driven from the timing gear. In the final year of production it was moved to a position in front of the engine and chain driven.

In the first year of the 11.50 and also in the last two years of the o.h.v. 680, there was the option of the old-type hinged rear fork spring frame. In the case of the larger model it meant an SS 100 type exhaust system with separate silencers in place of the characteristically massive 11.50 silencer. At this time, too, a new fork, the Brampton Monarch bottom link, was introduced, first on the short-lived o.h.v. 500 and then on the 11.50 although the Castle fork was an optional extra. The Brampton fork used the bottom links of the Castle but instead of the telescopic springing up top the sliders were replaced by a conventional girder fork link and a single central spring. It gave a softer ride and was popular for sidecar work.

Mention of sidecars brings us to another chapter of B.S. history. Sidecars specially adapted to suit Broughs had been offered from the earliest days but they were made by specialized sidecar manufacturers to B.S. requirements ... the most elaborate

being one for the pivoted-fork spring-frame models. This had the sidecar wheel linked to the sprung portion of the frame to stop roll. In 1938, however, G. B. announced the Alpine Grand Sports chassis ... popularly known as the petrol-tube chassis. Petrol tube because the endless 2in tube which formed the basis of the chassis, sweeping over the body at the front and enclosing it like a car bumper at the back, was used to carry spare petrol ... about 1½ gallons which could be pumped into the saddle tank by pressure from the tyre pump. Long half elliptic springs gave a luxurious ride to the launch or sports bodies fitted, and the wheel with knock-out spindle was enclosed in a tubular cradle. Verily a magnificent sidecar worthy of a B.S. .... the catalogue with typical reserve described it as a " Masterpiece of Design." Had the Dream materialized, it would have had a special chassis with two-point fitting and torsion-bar suspension.

In conclusion my sincere thanks to George Brough, Ike Webb, E. O. Blacknell, Arthur Birch and S. Campbell for their B.S. memoirs and to Barry Robinson for his painstaking research into the official records.   C. E. ALLEN

"B.S." Alpine Grand Sports Sidecar

This entirely new Brough Superior Sidecar is manufactured in my own factories. This masterpiece is patented throughout the world, and has been supplied in large numbers since its introduction two years ago, with every satisfaction to owners. Excellent results prove that my experience and decision in marketing this chassis, the main member of which consists of one large diameter *endless* tube, is fully justified. There are no brazed joints to cause crystallisation and consequent breakages. The body is underslung and carried on two long, flat, car-type leaf springs ; the quickly detachable wheel is properly housed in a tubular cradle frame ; as is also the car-type mudguard. The Single Frame Tube is utilised as a spare petrol container — it holds 1½ gallons — very useful on a long night journey.

Brough Superior ALPINE GRAND SPORTS SIDECAR (CRUISER BODY)
PATENT N. 413/239

Price
£32 " Cruiser " Body
£30 " Sports " Body